kamera
BOOKS

D1613208

James Gracey

DARIO ARGENTO

This edition published in 2010 by Kamera Books
PO Box 394, Harpenden, Herts, AL5 1XJ
www.kamerabooks.com

Copyright © James Gracey 2010
Series Editor: Hannah Patterson

ISBN 978-1-84243-318-8

2 4 6 8 10 9 7 5 3 1

Typeset by Elsa Mathern
Printed and bound in Great Britain by JF Print, Sparkford, Somerset

For my Father and Mother

ACKNOWLEDGEMENTS

Thanks to Mum, Dad, Scott and Chloe for all the smiling and nodding as I endlessly enthused about all things Argento.

From the bottom of my ventricles I would also like to thank the following people for endless encouragement, eye rolling and proof-reading abilities of the highest order: Emma Kelly, John McAliskey, Caroline Ryder, Alastair Crawford, Lucy Wood, John Kerr Mitchell, Craig Smith, Terri McManus and Shauneen Magorrian, all of whom also successfully managed to avoid watching anything that even re-motely resembled an Italian horror film throughout the course of this project – which was no mean feat! Thank you so much guys.

Thank you to the following for all their support: Christine Make-peace and Dylan Santurri at *Paracinema* magazine, Amber Wilkinson at Eye for Film and Francis Jones, Jonny Tiernan and all at AU.

'Diolch yn fawr' Ernest Mathijs and Mikel Koven, for sharing an in-clination towards the darker side of cinema and corrupting the mind of a simple slasher-movie fan. Thanks also to Vikkie Taggart, for intro-ducing me to ALL the Dario Argento fans and to Michael Bugajer for his helpful suggestions.

I'd also like to express my sincere gratitude to Sean Keller, Corali-na Cataldi-Tassoni and Marco Werba for their valuable time, insight and generosity.

Last, but certainly not least, many thanks to Anne Hudson for all her guidance and advice, and to Ion Mills and Hannah Patterson for providing me with the opportunity to write about one of my favourite filmmakers.

Sanguis Gratia Artis!

CONTENTS

INTRODUCTION: SYMPHONIES IN RED

For over 40 years now the breathtakingly violent and stylish films of Dario Argento have been shocking and terrifying audiences around the world. To watch an Argento film is to indulge in a totally visceral experience. Elaborate set pieces and dazzling cinematic artistry collide in a cacophony of blood and sinew. The camera is used like a weapon, ceaselessly prowling for its prey. Strange point-of-view shots align the viewer with both pursued and pursuer, implicating the audience in each ostentatious depiction of murder and mayhem. Attractive female victims glance back longingly as they flee in abstract terror, all too aware of their own vulnerability. At times almost sensual, each murder is filmed as though it were something more closely aligned with a sex scene; a frenzy of flesh and blood, culminating in a disturbing orgasm of bloody chaos. Lashings of bizarre and fetishistic images abound in Argento's work. One such recurring image is that of the killer's hands, clad in black leather gloves, fondling various sharp implements of death. The fact that Argento's own hands usually stand in for the killer's in these shots adds an additional dimension of perversity. Argento utilises images and sound, the very language of cinema, to further his twisted narratives in which logic is all but lost in a constant bombardment of nightmarish and extravagant style.

Argento is often referred to as 'the Italian Hitchcock' as he has made a name for himself creating scenes of terror and tension. Though Hitchcock's work is marked by its staunch linearity, focused plotting, narrative and logic, in Dario Argento's films these are often usurped in favour of atmosphere, technical prowess and provocative imagery.

Dario Argento was born in Rome on 7 September 1940. His father Salvatore was a well-respected and highly successful film producer integral to the international promotion of Italian cinema. Argento's mother Elda Luxardo was a famous and influential photographer. The young Argento grew up in the film industry surrounded by the rich and the beautiful – one of his earliest memories was of sitting on Sophia Loren's lap.

Argento, a sickly child, was condemned to spend long hours in bed. As a result, he became an avid reader and indulged in such works as *One Thousand and One Nights*, Shakespeare and, perhaps most significantly, Edgar Allan Poe. It was through Poe's vivid and feverish writing that Argento was first introduced to notions of death, the absurd and the mechanics of terror. Young Argento also loved to watch films, and it was as a youngster that he first viewed Lon Chaney in *The Phantom of the Opera* (1925). Unbeknownst to him, he would revisit the themes and indeed craft his own versions of this classic in much later life.

After graduating from high school and refusing to go to college, Argento worked for the Rome daily *Paese Sera* as a film critic. This, coupled with his father's profession and a brief dabble in acting, instilled within Argento an enviable knowledge of all things cinematic.

Italian cinema was resplendent and in the midst of its 'Golden Years' during the sixties and seventies when Argento entered its arena.

Starting off strong at the beginning of the twentieth century, Italy was producing historical epics and utilising custom-built sets for its films before anyone else. Sensational scenes of violence and decadence echoed the country's own illustrious and excessive history, with a rich past full of fantastical mythology to mine; it was inevitable that horror would find a home here. However, in the twenties Mussolini's Fascists seized power and established Cinecittà, which at the time was one of the world's most renowned and prolific production companies. Much of its output, though, until the fall of Mussolini in 1943, was given over to propagandist films.

Italian cinema had found its feet again by the sixties and it marked its return with a vengeance. Spaghetti Westerns had arrived, bringing high art and exploitative violence with them. Indeed, Argento's first major break came with an invitation from Sergio Leone to co-write (along with Bernardo Bertolucci) the epic masterpiece *Once Upon a Time in the West* (1968). This was at the age of 20. In Leone, Argento discovered a kindred spirit, a man who also thought and reasoned in images. His contribution to Leone's screenplay would open many doors for Argento but it would be a few years more before he decided to direct one of his own scripts.

Also amongst the rabble of new directors on the Italian film scene were two that would have a profound effect on Argento.

Riccardo Freda directed a number of films that Argento has claimed had an immense impact on him, including the dark and disturbing *L'Orribile segreto del Dr Hichcock/The Terror of Dr Hichcock* (1962), in which a doctor sedates his wife in order to indulge his necrophilic desires, resulting in tragedy, and *Lo spettro/The Ghost* (1963), a perverse tale of revenge and dark desire. Even more of an influence, though, was the work of one of Italy's most distinguished genre directors: Mario Bava.

Bava's films were imbued with a distinct Gothic ambience, and it was he who would bring Italian horror into the modern age, setting his bloodied stories against the backdrops of fashion houses and bustling cosmopolitan cities. His work boasted a myriad of elaborate deaths and violence, all cut through with a distinct style and flamboyance that would eventually bleed onto Argento's own filmic canvas. Bava single-handedly provided the blueprint for the *giallo* film with his films *The Girl Who Knew Too Much* (1963), widely regarded as the first *giallo* film, and *Blood and Black Lace* (1964).

GIALLO

Argento is famed for his lurid *giallo* films. *Giallo* (plural: *gialli*) is Italian for 'yellow' and the name originates from the trademark yellow covers of pulp crime-thriller paperback books that were extremely popular in Italy. Their literary counterparts were American hardboiled detective fiction by the likes of Raymond Chandler and Dashiell Hammett. When the work of crime and mystery writers such as Agatha Christie and Cornell Woolrich were first published in Italy they were marketed as *gialli*.

In cinematic terms the *giallo* is rather akin to the French 'noir' film in that it has many identifiable traits and conventions and is easily recognised by a distinctive visual grammar, much in the same way as 'slasher' films, for instance. The *giallo* certainly predates the slasher and had an overwhelming influence on it.

Giallo films notoriously combine sex and violence, hyper-stylised and elaborate murders, lavish camerawork and set design, displaced protagonists who unwittingly stumble into the ensuing mayhem, ineffectual or nonexistent police and copious gore. Fashion plays a significant role too, especially in the killer's fetishistic wardrobe of black leather gloves, dark raincoat and hat. Often the killer will have weighty psychological hang-ups. Everything weaves together in a weak and often convoluted narrative, frequently interrupted by scenes of startling violence and bloodshed. More abstract modes of detection are utilised rather than the usual logical deduction of 'whodunit'-style movies.

In the seventies and eighties, the genre was rife throughout the cinemas of Italy, shocking audiences with its combination of exploitative violence and stylish chic.

Argento would pick up the baton from Mario Bava and essentially do for the *giallo* what John Carpenter did for the slasher film with *Halloween* (1978). Following in the footsteps of Bava, Argento firmly cemented the popularity of the embryonic *giallo* flick, marking it with his own inimitable style and blood-soaked grandeur. Argento is one of the few directors working in cinema today, particularly horror cinema, who still retains full control over his work. Were it not for those pesky censors, of course, Argento would answer to no one.

AESTHETICS OF BLOOD

Allegations of misogyny have been hurled at Argento with great gusto since the beginning of his career. Film critic Mark Le Fanu once stated that Argento was preoccupied with 'devising novel and increasingly nasty ways of killing his female characters'.[1] However, this is an oversimplification of Argento's work, ignoring the director's fierce intellectualism, grasp of filmic language and technicality, and overlooking the fact that men aren't any safer in an Argento movie, though their deaths aren't filmed as longingly.

Other directors accused of misogyny have at least attempted to defend their work. For example Brian De Palma, whose earlier films such as *Dressed to Kill* (1980) and *Body Double* (1984) were labelled misogynistic, has stated:

> Women in peril works better in the suspense genre. It all goes back to *The Perils of Pauline* (1914). If you have a haunted house and you have a woman walking around with a candelabrum, you fear more for her than you would for a husky man.[2]

However, Argento has never appeared to openly defend himself. When he makes statements such as, 'I like women, especially beautiful ones; if they have a good face and figure, I would much prefer to watch them being murdered than an ugly girl or man'[3] he doesn't seem to be attempting to allay such criticism. This perhaps fits in more with Argento's aesthetic and painterly approach to his work and his affinity with the female form. If one looks carefully at his work, while it undeniably features bountiful images of beautiful women being stalked and slain, gender politics have never been straightforward. Men are killed with equal abandon and Argento has joked that he is an 'equal-opportunities killer'. In Argento's work, the age-old stereotype of women as the weaker, fairer and therefore more vulnerable sex is utilised as much as it is subverted. His films are headed by strong female characters. The killers are quite often women defending or avenging themselves against malicious masculinity. This opens up yet more labyrinthine avenues of ambiguity and sexual intrigue.

What adds even more fuel to the allegations of misogyny levelled at Argento is his audacious casting of partner Daria Nicolodi and daughter Asia in frequent roles. Argento and Nicolodi embarked on a passionate and often stormy relationship when they shot *Deep Red*. Their relationship resulted in some of Argento's greatest works. Nicolodi initially acted as a muse for the director – however, their relationship wasn't without its darker moments. Critics have suggested that it is possible to trace the disintegration of this relationship throughout Argento's films.

While appearing as a radiant heroine in *Deep Red*, the characters Nicolodi would later portray all met with increasingly violent and bloody deaths. In *Inferno* she portrays a neurotic and timid woman torn to pieces by demonic cats in an eerily blue-lit attic. While she survives events in *Tenebrae* she is not unscathed and her character is pushed to the brink of insanity. In *Phenomena* she is hacked to pieces by a cut-throat, razor-wielding chimpanzee. *Opera* would mark the last time they would work together for many years. In this film Nicolodi is shot through the head while looking through the peephole of a door. In typical Argento style, the camera follows the bullet in slow motion through her eye and out the back of her head as she is hurtled backwards through the air in slow motion. In their most recent reunion in the conclusion of Argento's 'Three Mothers' trilogy, *Mother of Tears*, Nicolodi appears as a spectral mother providing advice for her daughter from beyond the grave.

This problematic relationship between Dario and Daria seems to have been revisited a number of times by Argento in his onscreen relationship with his daughter, Asia. Adding to the somewhat disturbing and distinctly Freudian undertones already evident in his work, Argento has directed his daughter in a number of films where her characters are drugged, raped, beaten and only narrowly avoid being murdered. What is apparent, though, is that father and daughter have collaborated on films that stand out in both their careers as edgy, powerful, problematic and utterly compelling works.

With Asia killing off her mother, albeit onscreen, in *Scarlet Diva*, it would appear that the Argento clan work out their issues and exorcise relationships through their work; in front of cinema audiences and in fiendishly violent ways.

It's interesting to note that Argento's other daughter Fiore didn't fare much better when she appeared onscreen in *Demons*, *Phenomena* and *The Card Player* (she prefers to work behind the camera). It has also been suggested that Argento's relationship with his mother was fraught with strife, hence his Hitchcockian obsession with the monstrous maternal figures that lurk in many of his films.

All this speculation only adds to the absurd and macabre reputation Argento has cultivated for himself in his exploration of the darker side of human nature and catharsis of dark thoughts. At times it appears he relishes it.

EXQUISITE DEATH

Argento has been influenced by an almost encyclopaedic array of literature, art, philosophy and indeed cinema. It is the morbid writing of Edgar Allan Poe, however, that Argento has specifically cited as a major influence on his work. It may come as no surprise when viewing Argento's films and the very precise way he sexualises the victims and perpetrators within his work to discover that Poe was also preoccupied with sex and death and the shadowy realm where the two are locked in a twisted embrace. Poe claimed in his essay 'The Philosophy of Composition':

> I asked myself – of all melancholy topics, what, according to the universal understanding of mankind, is the most melancholy? Death was the obvious reply. And when, I said, is this the most melancholy of topics most poetical?
> When it most closely allies itself to beauty: the death then of a beautiful woman is unquestionably the most poetical topic in the world.

It is in this fascination with the 'aesthetics of death' that Argento is most closely aligned with Edgar Allan Poe. Argento himself has said:

> On reading Poe as a child it disturbed me and left me, for a long time, feeling strange and slightly sad… When I began to make films, I recognised that my themes had some affinity with the events told by Poe in his stories, his hallucinatory worlds, his bloody visions… In my solitary moments when some frightening idea strikes me and I think: with this I will make a film – Poe's handsome and intense face watches me, warns me to pay heed, to be careful.[4]

Perhaps it is simply an interest in women and an Edgar Allan Poe-inspired morbidity – and investigating how the two work when unified – that have propelled Argento along his trajectory of sex and death. Regardless, it is obvious that Argento is compelled, to use Jungian terminology, to gaze deep into the dark mirror of the psyche and peer at the uncanny things that live in its depths. This swirling of sex and death is lured into even darker, deadlier territory by Argento who once remarked:

> In such an intense physical act as murder, a very sensitive, somehow deeply erotic relationship is established somewhere

between the killer and his victim. There is something unifying between these acts, an erotic act and a bloodthirsty act… the orgasm of death and the sexual orgasm.[5]

This seems to reiterate the notion that Argento draws influence from the world of art and literature and, as stylish as his films are, they certainly don't lack subtextual meaning; in fact they lend themselves quite well to critical analysis. One only has to look at the depiction of women and death in the images created by the painters of the Renaissance – graphic and passionate representations of the melancholy and ecstatic deaths of women, such as Hans Baldung's 'Death and the Woman' – to see where Argento's influences stem from.

This amalgam of art, death and violence was also commented on by director Lucio Fulci when he dryly declared 'violence is Italian art'. Indeed, Italy's past is soaked in blood and glory and it is celebrated in its art and culture rather than reviled. The great Italian Renaissance artists such as Michelangelo, Da Vinci and Caravaggio created baroque and majestic works of art celebrating the volatility of their heritage. The darkly romantic texts of Boccaccio and Dante revel in hellish descriptions of live burials and descents into Hell. Opera, too, is deeply passionate and contains violent outbursts and perverse love and death. The voyeuristic impulse to watch scenes of violence is thousands of years old – public execution, anyone? Roman gladiators? Boxing?

Early Italian cinema also excelled in pushing the boundaries of sex and violence: Francesca Bertini was arguably the first bona fide star of cinema to appear partly naked on screen. The Italian historical epics and sword-and-sandal films were amongst the first to depict full-scale bloody battles and intimate close-ups of gory deaths. Spaghetti Westerns and *gialli* followed suit, ensuring Italian movies became almost synonymous with violence, sex and glorified death. Zombie and cannibal films by the likes of Lucio Fulci and Ruggero Deodato would embrace and intensify this preoccupation with striking images of abject terror and bloodshed.

Author of *Violence in the Arts*, John Frazer, has commented that:

> It is in violent encounters that one is required most obviously
> to reaffirm or reassess one's own values and to acknowledge
> the necessity of having as strong and clearly articulated a value
> system, as sharply defined a self, as much alertness to others
> and as firm a will as possible.

Despite the criticism his films receive for their violence, Argento still continues to explore violence and dark deeds, exposing the weakness of values and morality and struggling against established conventions throughout his blood-splattered oeuvre. Quentin Tarantino, another purveyor of violent movies who was heavily influenced by Argento, once said: 'As a filmmaker, when you deal with violence you are actually penalised for doing a good job.'[6]

As a result, Argento has become the epitome of everything audiences love and hate so much about Italian cinema; his stylish scenes of death and mayhem are amongst the most shocking in the history of cinema.

OPERATIC EXCESSES

This stylisation, verging on the pornographic, of violence and death is one of the main traits associated with the films of Dario Argento. At times, the director uses an expressionist style, revealing the influence on him of the likes of FW Murnau and Fritz Lang. Inner feelings of dread and anxiety are expressed outwardly through the set design, lighting and camerawork. Symbolic potential is exploited at the expense of cinematographic realism. Maitland McDonagh, author of *Broken Mirrors/Broken Minds: The Dark Dreams of Dario Argento* has stated that watching an Argento film is like having a 'vivid and complicated nightmare from which you can't wake up'.[7]

Two of Argento's most revered and startling films, *Suspiria* and *Inferno*, are supernatural horror flicks that play out like cruelly dark and twisted fairytales. Vivid colours and beautiful lighting simply drip out of each frame and an ever-present sheen of livid red lighting devilishly presides over proceedings. Extreme colours and overwrought images are all characteristic of 'vintage Argento'. While stylistically different from Argento's *gialli* films, they are no different when it comes to presenting scenes of violence and death.

Argento's ever-prowling camera haunts his entire body of work, showing the viewer everything in exquisite and gory detail. Images of beautiful women tiptoeing around vast buildings alone at night while curtains billow in an eerie breeze contain hefty sexual undertones. The sexual connotations are often as over-the-top as the murder sequences. Audiences are further manipulated and even disorientated by Argento's jagged editing techniques. Often cutting from extreme close-ups to wide-angle shots and point-of-view shots, the viewer is immersed in a kind of visual delirium, constantly on edge due to the fact that it is apparent anything can happen and potential danger lurks in the corner of every shot.

Never one to be satisfied simply trying to repeat past glories, Argento likes to forge ahead experimentally and defy expectation as he goes. Like many auteurs, Argento surrounds himself with people he trusts. Much like Lynch or Cronenberg, he collaborates with the same people time and again and, whilst his films may vary in style and, indeed, quality, there is a definite organic evolvement.

Despite his reputation and being a household name in his native Italy, much of his recent output has gone straight to video/DVD elsewhere. Argento has amassed a huge cult following, however, and his fans can be as scathing as critics when it comes to each new film. Harking back to the director's 'golden era' in the seventies and eighties, they are constantly longing for a 'return to form'. Argento has never been one to give in to what is expected, though, and fiercely continues to develop and experiment with widely different approaches to his bloody subject matter. Rather than complete his proposed 'Three Mothers' trilogy at the height of his popularity, Argento chose to return to the *giallo* with his next film *Tenebrae*.

Ever ahead of the pack, Argento utilises the most cutting-edge equipment and technology to enhance his dark visions: he was the first director to use CGI in Italy with *The Stendhal Syndrome*. In casting international stars – and, until recently, his films were always made without sound so actors could be dubbed in post-production – it is obvious that Argento has always aimed to appeal to a wide audience with a view to internationally distributing his work. The dubbing in many of his films, while initially distracting, doesn't really detract from the overall experience; in fact, if anything, it adds an uncanny and slightly creepy sheen to proceedings.

DREAMING IN RED: A BLOODY LEGACY

The influence Argento's films have had on horror cinema, particularly American slasher movies, is overwhelming. In one of the earliest examples of this subgenre, Bob Clarke's *Black Christmas* (1974), there are nods aplenty to Argento: the lurid lighting, stalking camerawork, close-ups of prying eyes and the use of an ornate crystal unicorn as the means to a bloody end. John Carpenter found much inspiration too in the likes of *Deep Red* and *Suspiria* and craftily paid homage to Argento with *Halloween* (1978), a film considered to be *the* seminal slasher film. Carpenter also plunders Argento's use of insects as agents of telepathy and harbingers of doom in his underrated *Prince of Darkness* (1987). Even Martin Scorsese was affected by the work of Argento when he directed *After Hours* (1985), with its series of increasingly nightmarish set pieces and logic-defying narrative progression. Numerous shots of people wandering down empty and eerily lit corridors and streets easily recall the work of Argento.

It would appear that with the proposed remake of *Suspiria* (something Argento is adamant he has nothing to do with), the long-awaited conclusion to his revered 'Three Mothers' trilogy finally completed, and his current film, simply entitled *Giallo*, boasting a cast of credible big names such as Adrien Brody and Emmanuelle

Seigner, Argento is experiencing something of a revival. Audiences are interested in his work: revisiting past glories and reappraising initially misunderstood works.

In the breakout indie hit *Juno* (2007), various characters discuss the work of Dario Argento and debate the merits of Argento and Herschell Gordon Lewis, the title character stating, 'Dario Argento is *so* the master of horror.' Lucky McKee's haunting and melancholy *May* (2002) unfolds as a loving homage to Argento. Rodman Flender's cult hit *Idle Hands* (1999) also wears its Argento influences on its bloodied sleeve, as does Katsuhiro Ôtomo's *Phenomena*-tinged *Mushishi* (2006), as it follows the exploits of a mystical doctor who uses his telepathic link with insects to conquer evil forces. French director Pascal Laugier even went so far as to dedicate his unflinchingly intense art-house shocker *Martyrs* (2008) to Dario Argento.

It is not just 'cult' filmmakers that emulate Argento, though. Quentin Tarantino pays homage to Argento in the scene in *Death Proof* (2007) when we are introduced to the second group of female characters as they stroll through a car park, unaware they are being photographed by the perverted Stuntman Mike. The scene is accompanied by the strains of Morricone's music for *The Bird with the Crystal Plumage*; airy, sexy and tinged with danger. Indeed, Tarantino nods as much to Argento as he does Samurai movies in *Kill Bill: Vol 1* (2003) when Sophie has her arm lopped off in a geyser of blood à la *Tenebrae*. Argento's hip and cult status has been sealed. Even a stage musical of *Deep Red* has begun its tour of Italy!

With a renewed interest in Argento's movies, audiences are now viewing them from a fresh angle and in the context of their influence on the likes of Quentin Tarantino et al. With his latest offering, the director looks set to introduce his beloved *giallo* movies to a whole new generation, tired of remakes and re-imaginings.

With the recent revival of extreme violence and brutal torture in the horror genre as exemplified by the likes of base cinematic experiences *Hostel* (2005) and *The Devil's Rejects* (2005), sometimes nicknamed 'torture/horror-porn', Argento's brand of terror is still shrouded in a tapestry of Gothic elegance and highly sexualised fervour. It plays out in a different arena of punishment where the violence is just as brutal but the presentation more considered and opulent, even lyrical. Argento continues to create feverishly violent films with a level of artistry rarely seen in horror cinema.

Argento once said, 'I am in love with the colour red. I dream in red. My nightmares are dominated by red. Red is the colour of passion and the colour of the journey into our subconscious. But above all, red is the colour of fear and violence.'[8]

He has also playfully remarked in many interviews that after making all these films, he would 'probably be a good killer'.[9]

While he is still dreaming in red, we will no doubt bear witness to more of Dario Argento's frenzied, lurid and nightmarish compositions of exquisite and ecstatic deaths, rife with a morbid and dark sensuality, for some time to come. And, as you are reading this book, I am sure you will agree with me that this is not a bad thing at all.

THE ANIMAL TRILOGY

L'Uccello dalle piume di cristallo/
The Bird with the Crystal Plumage (1970)

'Bring out the perverts.'

Directed/Written by: Dario Argento
Produced by: Salvatore Argento
Music by: Ennio Morricone
Cinematography: Vittorio Storaro
Edited by: Franco Fraticelli
Production Design: Dario Micheli
Cast: Tony Musante (Sam Dalmas), Suzy Kendall (Julia), Enrico Maria Salerno (Inspector Morosini), Eva Renzi (Monica Ranieri), Umberto Raho (Alberto Ranieri), Raf Valenti aka Renato Romano (Professor Carlo Dover)
Also known as: *The Gallery Murders, Phantom of Terror, Bird with Glass Feathers*

Synopsis

American writer Sam Dalmas is temporarily residing in Italy attempting to find a solution to his writer's block. Wandering home one evening, he passes by an art gallery and witnesses a struggle between a woman and an unidentifiable figure. Rushing to try and help the woman, Sam becomes trapped between two sets of glass doors and helplessly looks on as the assailant stabs the woman and then flees, leaving her to writhe in agony on the floor of the gallery. Sam relays to the police what he saw, though he can't help but think that he has forgotten a key piece of information. The police believe the attacker was also responsible for a bout of recent murders and, with their encouragement, Sam sets about trying to uncover the mystery and find the killer, putting his own life and that of his girl-friend in grave danger.

Background

Dario Argento wrote *The Bird with the Crystal Plumage* for himself, loosely basing it on a Fredric Brown novel called *The Screaming Mimi*.

He had grown tired of seeing his previous screenplays get handed over to directors he thought were less than competent at turning his words into images and, having enjoyed the various thriller aspects in his prior scripts, Argento was interested in expanding these ideas into a full-length feature and investigating the machinery of fear. He wanted to create a *noir*-type mystery thriller set in Rome, something that was quite uncommon at the time, with the exception of Mario Bava's *The Girl Who Knew Too Much* (1963) and *Blood and Black Lace* (1964), both released almost a decade before. With a $500,000 budget, filming began in August 1969.

The cast features Tony Musante, who had previously starred in the Argento-penned *The Love Circle* (1969). Something of an egotist, it is reputed that Argento's tentative relationship with actors stems from his experiences working with Musante: amongst other things, the wayward actor allegedly telephoned Argento many times in the early hours demanding character 'motivation'. Suzy Kendall, who had previously appeared in *Circus of Fear* (1966) with Christopher Lee, portrays Sam's girlfriend Julia.

Goffredo Lombardo, the head of Titanus Studios, was impressed with Argento's previous work as a writer and agreed to give him the chance to direct *The Bird with the Crystal Plumage*. Lombardo hated the early rushes he saw and even wanted to replace Argento, but was convinced by the director and his producer father, Salvatore, to trust them to deliver.

So unconventional was the film that its preview for Titanus executives was something of a letdown. They thought it was too different and offbeat to become a hit and believed that, by showing the killer at the beginning of the film, Argento was being too progressive. It was only when Lombardo noticed how shaken his secretary was after viewing the film that he realised Argento's brand of horror might just do well at the box office. When the film opened, positive reviews and gradual word of mouth ensured that it went on to become a box-office success both in Europe and abroad.

Comments

The Bird with the Crystal Plumage features traits now commonly associated with Argento's body of films: the somewhat sketchy characterisation and wandering plot; spectacular techniques that exist for their own sake and don't contribute to driving forward the narrative but are simply used to astound the viewer; almost fetishised depictions of violence and death; a seemingly androgynous murderer garbed in a dark raincoat and black leather gloves; voyeurism and spectatorship; the misinterpretation of key events and the 'stranger abroad' protagonist. The plot and characters come second to style and atmosphere in an Argento film.

The titular bird refers to a rare Siberian specimen found in a zoo in Rome. Its bizarre call is heard in the background of a pivotal phone call from the killer to Sam, thus helping him track down the perpetrator.

Style/Technical

Argento has cited the work of Fritz Lang as a major influence on his own work, particularly in terms of editing and frame composition. A number of scenes in *The Bird with the Crystal Plumage*, particularly the ones set in the fog-cluttered streets of Rome after dark, echo similar nightmarish street scenes in Lang's disturbing *M* (1931).

The film was photographed by cinematographer Vittorio Storaro, who would go on to lens *Apocalypse Now* (1979). Utilising zoom and telephoto lenses, Storaro and Argento approached the film with an experimental spirit still evident today, and the film has a dazzlingly stylish look that influenced a slew of pale imitations.

Argento really shows his true colours in depicting the scenes of murder and mayhem. Such style and aplomb have rarely been glimpsed in the horror genre.

Unconventional editing techniques were also employed by Argento, resulting in some rather unnerving and disorientating effects. Frequently cutting from extreme close-ups to wide-angle shots, he conveys perfectly the sense of visual and aural fragmentation of an event slowly being pieced together.

The film is peppered with flashbacks to the scene in the gallery as Sam becomes obsessed with solving the case. These aren't signalled like traditional flashbacks, though; they are simply slotted into the narrative, resulting in an off-kilter and delirious pace of events.

Like the majority of Argento's work, *The Bird with the Crystal Plumage* was shot without sound, with a view to dubbing the film in post-production for the international market.

Themes

Voyeurism and spectatorship, major preoccupations of Argento's, are played out in *Bird* in scenes such as the one where Sam, trapped between the glass doors of the gallery, is forced to watch an attempted murder, and Julia, trapped in her apartment, helplessly looks on as the killer hacks through the door, very, very slowly. This forced spectatorship foreshadows the somewhat overtly sadistic forced gaze evident in *Opera* and it exquisitely highlights Argento's concerns with subverting the detached spectatorship of cinema audiences; essentially holding their fixed gaze in much the same way as the unfolding events hold the attention of the characters enveloped within them. The threat of violence is usually only a blink away in an Argento film. Quite literally in the case of *Opera*.

The main character is a writer, another familiar 'Argentoism'. He is in Rome to try and alleviate his writer's block and supports himself by writing rather dry research papers on zoology. As a direct result of the madness he is plunged into while trying to solve the case, his writer's block disappears and he feels rejuvenated, revelling in this chaos.

The ineffectual police are a mainstay of Argento's work. In fact, until *The Stendhal Syndrome*, *The Card Player* and *Giallo* we don't really follow the police in their investigations; the story is always based around the amateur sleuth, usually an artist of some kind, be they a musician, singer or writer.

Also evident are a number of oddball characters typically featured in Argento's early work: the crazed artist who exists on a diet of cats; the pimp with an amusingly unfortunate speech impediment; and the police line-up of sex perverts and a misplaced transvestite ('Ursula Andress belongs with the transvestites not the perverts' – Inspector Morosini).

Notions of gender are somewhat subverted in *The Bird with the Crystal Plumage* as the killer is revealed to be a woman undergoing a bizarre psychological transfer instigated by viewing a painting that reminds her of a long-repressed trauma. The fact that this traumatic event was also the inspiration for the artist who created the painting is indeed a key to unlocking the mystery.

Femininity is usually equated with passivity; thus when Sam sees Monica struggling with an unidentifiable figure he misinterprets what he is seeing – wrongly assuming that Monica is being attacked by a man and that she is the hapless victim. The overtly sexualised nature of the murders would also suggest a male killer; this highlights Argento's capacity for subverting conventions. The twist ending also relies on a similar presumption on the part of the audience. It is also significant that, during the struggle, Monica is dressed in white and her assailant decked out in black, typically representing good and evil respectively. While Monica is revealed to be the killer, she is also portrayed as a victim – the genesis of her psychosis stemming from having once been attacked by a man. This idea of psychological transfer and psychoanalysis is overtly Freudian and a common Hitchcock trait too.

The premise of a painting unlocking memories of a childhood trauma signifies Argento's preoccupation with art and its effects on the human psyche. The idea that art can be deadly is something of a recurring theme in his canon: Sam becomes trapped under a huge sculpture in the gallery and this precedes the notion of 'art as a weapon' used at the climax of *Tenebrae*. As Monica writhes around on the floor of the gallery, she is as much on display as the sparsely exhibited works of art around her. Indeed, the look of some of the art in her gallery reflects the themes of the film: a giant pair of sculpted talons highlights the relationship between predator and prey, killer and victim. This theme of 'art as dangerous' would also be revisited with a vengeance in *The Stendhal Syndrome*.

The paintings, photos, framing of shots and flashbacks are all methods of visual communication. The killer frequently photographs her victims before she dispatches them; similar actions are deployed by the killer in *Tenebrae*, who captures the deaths of his victims on camera, photo-journalist Rod Usher in Argento's segment of *Two Evil Eyes* and the perverted killer in *Giallo*.

The deceptive nature of 'vision' and perception is a common theme Argento explores throughout his work. His protagonists usually spend much of their time trying to remember something they've seen or heard. Elusive details that initially appeared irrelevant or were misinterpreted usually hold the key to solving the mystery. Argento also skews the usual logical deduction techniques used in detective thrillers by basing the unravelling of the mystery on the somewhat irrational and absurd narrative of a painting. This 'aesthetic' detection is not the usual clinical and rational method deployed. Sam utilises his artistic nature to unveil a series of concepts and ideas that reveal the culprit.

Music

Ennio Morricone's shimmering and hallucinatory jazz-inflected score has an irresistible mondo-kitsch appeal, with tantalising and alluring vocals by Edda dell'Orso. A gentle guitar strums over increasingly melancholic and lush strings, giving way to more abstract and sinister pieces used in the film's violent and tense moments.

Verdict

With his debut, Argento earned all sorts of comparisons with Hitchcock – *Variety* went so far as to dub him a 'garlic-flavoured Hitchcock' and *The Bird with the Crystal Plumage* went some way to bridging the gap between art-house and exploitation in Italian cinema. The plot is one of his tightest, yet overall the film lacks the grandiosity of later efforts. However, it acts as one of Argento's most accessible films and the perfect introduction to his work. Stylish, taut and unflinchingly intense.

Il Gatto a nove code/Cat O'Nine Tails (1971)

Directed/Written by: Dario Argento
Produced by: Salvatore Argento
Music by: Ennio Morricone
Cinematography: Erico Menczer
Edited by: Franco Fraticelli
Art Director: Carlo Leva
Optical Effects: Luciano Vittori
Cast: James Franciscus (Carlo Giordani), Karl Malden (Franco Arno), Catherine Spaak (Anna Terzi), Pier Paolo Capponi (Superintendent Spimi), Horst Frank (Dr Braun), Rada Rassimov (Bianca Merusi), Aldo Reggiani (Dr Casoni), Carlo Alighiero (Dr Calabresi)

Synopsis

Franco Arno and his young niece, Lori, overhear part of a conversation between two people in a parked car, their words implying blackmail. As Arno is blind, he asks Lori to discreetly describe the people in the car, but she can only see one of them clearly. Later that night, across the street from Arno's apartment, a security guard is knocked unconscious and a shadowy figure breaks into the Terzi Institute of Genetic Research. A series of murders prompts Arno and journalist Carlo Giordani to track down the killer, who has a strange obsession with the Institute. They begin to suspect that the mysterious research being carried out there holds the key to unlocking the killer's identity.

Background

Argento realised he had a distinct knack for creating scenes of terror and suspense. He wanted to move with the times and keep ahead of trends, trying something fresh that would defy the expectations of his viewers. Distributors were calling out for another *Bird with the Crystal Plumage* and, as a result, Argento felt pressurised – to the extent that he now believes he missed the point – in trying too hard to surprise audiences with his second film, he lost sight of his own vision.

Cat O'Nine Tails is actually Argento's least favourite among his own creations and, oddly enough, the only film he has made that has never been cut by censors.

With a budget of $1 million, twice that of *Bird*, Argento wrote the script with Luigi Collo and Dardano Sacchetti (who would later go on to work with Mario Bava and Lucio Fulci). The film's central concept of criminality being genetic was one that fascinated Argento. The idea that anyone has the potential to do evil things because of their genetic make-up, something they have no control over, is a rather disturbing one. This premise echoes an earlier British film, *Twisted Nerve* (1968), featuring a schizophrenic killer whose murderous behaviour is revealed to be the result of a sinister imbalance at chromosomal level.

Due to the success of *The Bird with the Crystal Plumage* in the States, Argento had a number of American co-producers and they insisted on the inclusion of James Franciscus on the cast roster. Franciscus was creating quite a stir at the time in films such as *Beneath the Planet of the Apes* (1970) and the Charlton Heston lookalike had some star power. Fellow American Karl Malden, who previously starred in *A Streetcar Named Desire* (1951), grasped the chance to play such a challenging role and his portrayal of Franco Arno is an extremely sensitive one. He and Franciscus have great chemistry and the duo beat together as the uncharacteristically warm heart of this Argento film. Indeed, Arno's relationship with his niece Lori is also curiously touching, if a little over-sentimental. It is because of the threat of violence to Lori that Arno kills Casoni, pushing him down an elevator shaft, his hands burning while he grips the cable on the way down. Even though the violence towards Lori is only implied at the end of *Cat O'Nine Tails*, violence towards children would rear its head sporadically throughout Argento's career, particularly in *Mother of Tears*.

Comments

At times Argento blends comedy with tension quite well, and this is evident in the barbershop and cemetery scenes. He also dabbles in outright comedy with greater success than he did in *The Five Days of Milan*. Such black humour occurs in the scene featuring an elderly couple attempting to cross the road during the slick car chase. Argento also reveals a somewhat morbid sense of humour with the shot of a dead character's car, its windshield cluttered with parking tickets, and in the shots of the lactating milk cartons during the tepid sex scene.

Argento also seems overly keen to forestall the unveiling of the killer – the film is awash with red herrings and it's as if he is saying to his audience that the point of the film is not to find out WHY these murders are occurring, but HOW.

Aside from *Giallo*, *Cat O'Nine Tails* is saddled with what is possibly one of Argento's bleakest and most downbeat endings. We don't know if order and equilibrium have been restored as we never see all of the characters together again; was Lori murdered and did Giordani die from his wounds? It is a cruel ambiguity and unsettling to the core. As Argento refuses to provide a satisfactory ending, events tend to linger in the mind afterwards and, in doing this, he is suggesting that, in reality, order isn't always restored after the solving of a crime – why should it be any different in movies?

While *Cat O'Nine Tails* didn't perform very well at the US box office, it has seen something of a revival more recently; critics now claim that it is an underrated entry in Argento's canon. This marks a significant difference to how it was originally received, with critics referring to it as, amongst other things, 'vomitous' and 'a flashy-stylish murder mystery' (Judith Crist, *New York Times*).

Style/Technical

The film opens with a long tracking shot along the roof of a tall city building, peering over the edge as it goes. It isn't made clear if what we see in this shot is aligned with a particular character's point of view or not, but it impresses nonetheless. Shots like this, that appear to exist only for the sake of looking impressive and don't really further the story, are a frequent motif in Argento's work.

There are a number of scenes that end and begin by briefly inter-cutting with each other, another trait of the director's earlier work, particularly evident in *Door into Darkness*. This creates a slick and smooth feel but often jolts the audience in moments of tension. For example, the scene featuring Arno mulling over a puzzle is intercut suddenly with almost subliminal shots of the Terzi Institute. These brief shots become more prolonged and with each one we move further into the Institute, until we finally cut permanently from Arno to the perspective of the killer inside the Institute. Until we realise what's occurring, one could assume that this style of editing is signifying a flashback of some sort. The result is disorientating and disarming.

A similar scene involving Arno and Lori discussing Calabresi's death and deciding to go and see Giordani contains gradually longer shots of Giordani in his office, until eventually we cut permanently to his office as Arno and Lori show up.

The editing technique utilised in *Cat O'Nine Tails* follows on from *The Bird with the Crystal Plumage*'s experimental style, racking up the tension and dizzying theatrical violence, bringing us up close and personal with the ensuing chaos.

Argento was visually inspired by Robert Siodmak's *The Spiral Staircase* (1945), a film following the exploits of a homicidal maniac stalking a blind woman and liberally sprinkled with close-up shots of a vast and blinking eye.

The camerawork in *Cat O'Nine Tails* is already beginning to resemble the type of fluid and ever-prowling characteristics that Argento is revered for. The director obviously relishes cranking up the tension by cutting back and forth from the perspective of the killer to that of the hopeless victim, again steadily pushing the limits of onscreen violence. At times, characters also address the camera directly and it appears as though they are addressing the audience, thus implicating us in the crime. The result is quite creepy and unnerving.

Argento also has a bit of fun with audience expectations in a line spoken by the photographer at the first murder scene – 'That's right, smile. Smile. A man is dead.' Is this Argento prodding the audience, as if to say 'this character died for your entertainment'?

With *Cat*, Argento proved that style and technical flamboyance were just as important to his work, if not more so, than the plot or characterisation; in fact, it could be argued that Argento finds scripts and narrative logic nothing but a hindrance to his creativity, grounding his agile pyrotechnics. The brutal violence that punctures the film was inspired by the bloodshed in Spaghetti Westerns; Argento wanted it raw and distressing. The film features a number of gratuitous strangulations and we are thrust so close up to the action that we can see the saliva in the gasping mouths of the victims.

The muted brown tones evident in the look of *Cat O'Nine Tails* echo the subdued palettes of *Trauma* and *Giallo* and, like these films, the violence is gritty and intense.

Themes

Close-up shots of the seemingly omniscient eye that gazes cruelly over proceedings marks the presence of the chromosomally challenged murderer and recalls themes of voyeurism and spectatorship in *The Bird with the Crystal Plumage*. We are constantly bombarded with images of eyes and references to eyes. At one point Braun, a rather suave scientist, compliments Giordani on his eyes and the photographer is murdered for 'seeing' too much, unintentionally capturing the killer in action with the eye of his camera.

Cat O'Nine Tails, however, subverts this idea of voyeurism in a cruel and somewhat ironic twist with the blindness of Franco Arno. He is one of Argento's most interesting characters, with his natural curiosity and finely tuned perception. Many of the characters within the film are essentially 'blind', though, as they are not willing to see the potential clues revealing who the killer is. It is ultimately Arno who uncovers key evidence that sets the investigation in motion. He deduces that Calabresi was murdered after Lori describes the photo of the man's fall beneath the train to him. He urges Giordani to seek out the original photo to see if it was cropped. This turns out to be the case and, at the edge of the photo, *Blow Up* (1966)-style, they make out an unidentified arm pushing Calabresi to his death.

While the investigation in this film is more grounded in logic than those of other Argento films, implausible and slightly absurd modes of detection still litter the script: Arno realises a clue to the killer's identity has been hidden in Bianca's locket simply because he hears a noise that reminds him of how she played with the locket's chain. Again, it would appear that rational methods of deduction have been sidestepped in favour of more abstract means of investigation.

The genetic research facility, the Terzi Institute, features heavily in the story and characters return there frequently looking for answers. The premise of a building harbouring deadly secrets mirrors Argento's later preoccupations with forbidden buildings such as the houses of the Three Mothers and the 'haunted' villas of *Deep Red* and *Sleepless*.

Characters with somewhat unsavoury and typically 'Argentoesque' traits populate *Cat O'Nine Tails*, with all manner of perverse deeds unfolding, including incest, murder (obviously), violence towards children, adultery and blackmail. Also worth mentioning and typical of early Argento are the oddball 'comedic' secondary characters such as Gigi the luckless burglar, and the cop obsessed with all-things-culinary.

This film is interesting and unusual for Argento because, instead of the usual Freudian psychoanalytical motivation on the killer's part, events are explained in cold and rational scientific terms. Casoni was being blackmailed because of his genetic imbalance and turned killer to prevent anyone ruining his career. It is suggested, though, that Casoni murdered, not exclusively because of his corrupt genes, but because he brooded too much about them. Argento subtly refers to corruption in the family, as Casoni inherited his genetic make-up, and therefore murderous tendencies, from his parents. This is a theme the director would visit time and again in the likes of *Four Flies on Grey Velvet*, *Deep Red*, *Phenomena*, *Opera*, *Trauma* and *Giallo*.

In an effective scene set in a crypt, involving the desecration of a grave and near premature interment of one of the characters, Argento nods to one of his major influences, Edgar Allan Poe, in his exploitation of primitive fears.

Music

Morricone's sparse and gracefully sinister score at times reaches shrill proportions, helping to create a taut atmosphere, full of menace and dread, aided by the dark and bizarrely constructed jazz improvisations. Typical of Morricone and the time in which he scored this film, the music has a chic and trendy lounge sound that accompanies Argento's gliding camera and perverse imagery. The cooing and melodic lullaby, a common musical motif throughout Argento's movie soundtracks, is sporadically interrupted by sudden clicks and clambering of percussion.

Trivia

The newspaper Giordani writes for, *Paese Sera*, is the newspaper Argento used to write for.

Verdict

With a number of well-staged set pieces, Argento is evidently equipped to oil the cogs of the 'mechanics' of suspense. A worthy follow-up to *The Bird with the Crystal Plumage*, *Cat O'Nine Tails* further showcases Argento's brand of chic mayhem. With heavy stylisation and a convoluted plot, we are again reminded of the traits that would become commonly associated with the cruel cinema of Argento.

4 mosche di velluto grigio/Four Flies on Grey Velvet (1971)

Directed/Written by: Dario Argento
Produced by: Salvatore Argento
Music by: Ennio Morricone
Cinematography: Franco Di Giacomo
Edited by: Françoise Bonnot
Production Design: Enrico Sabbatini

Special Effects: Cataldo Galiano
Cast: Michael Brandon (Roberto Tobias), Mimsy Farmer (Nina Tobias), Jean-Pierre Marielle (Gianni Arrosio), Marisa Fabbri (Amelia), Constanza Spada aka Laura Troschel (Maria), Francine Racette (Dalia), Bud Spencer aka Carlo Pedersoli (Godfrey)

Synopsis

After his rock band completes their practice session, drummer Roberto Tobias follows a man who has been stalking him to an abandoned theatre to confront him. During the confrontation there is a scuffle and the man falls lifelessly into the orchestra pit, stabbed with his own knife. This is all photographed by a mysterious figure wearing a sinister puppet mask hiding in the balcony.

The next morning Roberto receives the dead man's ID card in the mail. Photos of the event start showing up around his home and studio and Roberto grows increasingly paranoid as bodies begin to pile up and the mysterious figure lures him into a deadly game of cat and mouse.

Background

Cat O'Nine Tails had just broken even outside Italy. Like *The Bird with the Crystal Plumage*, though, it was received well at the Italian box office. The follow-up, *Four Flies on Grey Velvet*, was scripted by Argento, Mario Foglietti and Luigi Cozzi, a fan of Argento (and the first person to conduct an interview with the maestro about his career) who would go on to become a director of horror films himself. Argento's personal life was in turmoil at this stage in his career. He and his wife Marisa were in the midst of a divorce and he was living with his daughter Fiore.

The restlessness he felt perhaps contributed in some way to Argento's declaration that *Four Flies on Grey Velvet* would be his last *giallo*. Little did he know at this stage that the creative seeds planted by this film would later blossom into the bloody flower that is *Deep Red*.

Paramount picked up the rights to distribute *Four Flies on Grey Velvet* internationally; they were the first major studio to distribute an Argento film outside Italy, and were all too vocal in their concerns about Argento's casting choices, though they were satisfied when the leading role went to rising star Michael Brandon.

Comments

Four Flies on Grey Velvet marked the end of the first significant phase of Argento's long and bloody career. The style evident in the film was to become more pronounced in later work, the images more baroque and intense, and the narrative even more ambiguous.

Like *Cat O'Nine Tail*'s murderous chromosomes, it features another bizarre and somewhat convoluted scientific quirk to further along the meandering plot: a device that is able to capture the last image processed by a dead person's eyes. The special effects were created by Cataldo Galiano. Interestingly, Argento had initially considered utilising the talents of Carlo Rambaldi who would later help create the effects used in *ET* (1982) and *King Kong* (1976) and eventually work with Argento on *Deep Red*.

Four Flies on Grey Velvet would feature a return to Freudian subtext after the scientific motives in *Cat O'Nine Tails* and Argento would draw on the likes of Hitchcock's *Torn Curtain* (1966) and various Val Lewton-produced horror pictures, particularly Jacques Tourneur's *The Leopard Man* (1943). Produced during a period when the *giallo* had really become popular and cinemas throughout Italy were saturated with absurd and beautifully titled films (*Five Dolls for an August Moon* (1970), *A Lizard in Woman's Skin* (1971), *Don't Torture a Duckling* (1972), *Short Night of the Glass Dolls* (1971), *The Case of the Bloody Iris* aka *What Are These Strange Drops of Blood on the Body of Jennifer?* (1972) and *Your Vice is a Locked Room and Only*

I Have the Key (1972), to name but a few!), Argento was really at the forefront of this popularity, his first two films having ignited the trend. If anything, the influence he had on other filmmakers urged him to forge ahead, try to do the unexpected and break moulds with his own particular brand of thriller.

Style/Technical

Argento's stylish techniques are evident from the get-go in *Four Flies*. The opening title sequence alone is a veritable tour-de-force of rapid editing, obscure camera angles and directorial chutzpah, featuring shots of Tobias's rock band rehearsing, intercut with shots of an exposed beating heart on a black background, anticipating the heart-thumping tension to come.

Argento's 'camera as killer' would really come into play in this film. Several times throughout the twisting story, the audience are aligned with the killer as we view events from their perspective. When the killer experiences flashbacks to a childhood trauma, the camera glides into a padded cell and begins a dizzying 360-degree spin, suggesting the frenzied anguish of the tortured killer.

Argento, ever experimental, utilised a high-speed camera that shot 1,000 frames per second, as opposed to the usual 24 frames per second. This is employed to startling effect during the devastating and strangely poignant climactic slow-motion car crash, in which Nina is decapitated and the shards of broken glass seem to float around her ethereally in their own brief cosmos of beautiful destruction.

In the scene where Roberto is shot in the arm, the camera follows the bullet as it fires from the gun, predating *The Matrix* (1999) and Argento's own *Opera* and *The Stendhal Syndrome*, where similar effects would be deployed for dramatic effect.

Another bravura sequence occurs when the housekeeper Maria telephones the killer and Argento lets loose his camera to rise above the phone booth, snake around the cables, traverse the phone wire,

dive beneath the streets, shoot through a switchboard along more wires, and come out the other end at the killer's phone. This rather unnecessary but technically impressive series of shots showcases the sinister aspects of a phone call: the fact that a voice from any-where in the world can be heard in your ear across all that space and time is rendered unnerving and threatening.

Argento also employs similar methods of jump-cutting and edit-ing as he did in *The Bird with the Crystal Plumage* and *Cat O'Nine Tails*. When Roberto is driving to the office of his private investigator we cut between him in his car and shots of the PI's building. The cuts to the building gradually follow the camera up the stairs and along corridors, until we permanently cut to Roberto walking into the office himself. These shots serve to stylishly bridge diegetic barriers of time and space within the film.

Similar techniques are utilised in one of the most outstanding scenes in the film. Waiting in the park for her rendezvous with the killer, the housekeeper Maria sits on a bench smoking a cigarette. Her surroundings gradually begin to change, becoming darker and more foreboding – the children playing disappear, cavorting lovers in the bushes vanish and the absence of Morricone's score adds to the unnerving revelation of time passing unnoticed. When she snaps out of her daze Maria discovers she has been locked in the now deserted park with the killer. This echoes a similar scene in Tourneur's *The Leopard Man* (1943) where a young woman waits for her lover in a cemetery, smoking a cigarette and losing herself in her thoughts. She then realises that she has been locked in and is murdered. In what appears to be a direct homage to Lewton's understated and subtle brand of horror, Maria is also killed offscreen in *Four Flies*, an uncommon trait for Argento, at least until *The Card Player*'s relatively bloodless murders. The unreliability of what is presented as the character's point of view, and what we as an audi-ence realise is actually going on, recalls Sam's encounter between the glass doors in *The Bird with the Crystal Plumage*.

A similar auditory link is deployed when Roberto wakens from his sleeping nightmare, in which he hears the killer threatening him, into the actual nightmare of his real life to find the killer whispering in his ear – the result is bizarre and chillingly irrational.

Themes

Tobias is an interesting Argento protagonist. Typically, he is involved in the arts as a musician and is an 'outsider' living in Italy. However, unlike the previous sleuths in Argento's films, Roberto has not accidentally stumbled into this web of deceit and death because of something he has witnessed; instead, the killer is punishing him and relishing his suffering for reasons yet to be discovered. He is the sole cause of the murders occurring around him. When he purposefully confronts his stalker and seemingly stabs him to death, he sets in motion the dark plans Nina has for him. Roberto is quite an unsympathetic character; he possibly murdered his stalker and he seduced his wife's cousin. He also reminds Nina of her cruel and abusive father. His tender-footed investigation doesn't prompt her to murder again to silence him – she kills to torment him.

Critics have noted the physical similarities between Brandon and Argento, and have suggested that Roberto Tobias is perhaps one of Argento's earliest onscreen alter-egos. Interestingly, according to Luigi Cozzi, this was one of the only films in which Argento didn't appear as the killer. Cozzi himself played this role. Critics have suggested that this was due to Brandon fulfilling Argento's 'role' onscreen. Unlike other alleged Argento alter-egos, the director doesn't use Roberto to reflect any relevant opinions of his own as he does with Peter Neal in *Tenebrae* and Marco in *Opera*, whose discussions about misogyny and violence in cinema attempt to allay criticism aimed at Argento.

Four Flies is full of marginalised characters existing on the fringes of mainstream society, along with several oddball characters typically found in Argento's films: the American rock musician living in

43

Italy, the hermetic and raw-fish-eating God(frey), the gay private investigator and the deeply confused and internally tortured Nina.

Arrosio, the private investigator, while stereotypically gay, is sensitively portrayed by French actor Jean-Pierre Marielle, who actually improvised much of the character, including his sexual orientation. As a result, the character retains a certain humanity and credibility. He is not the only gay character in an Argento film (Professor Braun in *Cat O'Nine Tails*, Marta in *Mother of Tears* and Carlos in *Deep Red* are others), but he is certainly one of the most fleshed out and sympathetic. His presence adds a welcome light touch to the otherwise dark and macabre proceedings; and his sexuality is not his defining characteristic, merely one aspect of a carefully portrayed character.

The concepts of voyeurism and spectatorship are further explored in this film. Characters are often murdered in Argento's films because of what they observe and might uncover. In *Four Flies*, it is what they see and what is captured on their retina by a pseudo-scientific contraption that, after their death, will reveal the killer's identity. Interestingly, Depression-era gangsters would shoot out their victims' eyes in response to a superstition that clues to a person's killer could be found in them.

Argento's preoccupation with images and the visual is also further explored as the killer photographs Roberto in the empty theatre struggling with his stalker. These photos show up around Roberto's home and studio, reminding him that someone is watching his every move. It is also a photograph that gives Arrosio his first clue to the killer's identity and motivation when he notices a shocking similarity between two people.

Unusually for an Argento film, there is a faint religious subtext. A character named God shows up just in time to 'save' Roberto from the killer, and throughout the film they have conversations about faith and death. Apart from this and several shots in *The Church*, *The Stendhal Syndrome* and *Mother of Tears*, allusions to religion are markedly absent from Argento's oeuvre. His characters exist in a coldly godless universe, living and dying alone, the victims of pure chance.

The gender-confusion and physicality of the characters in *Four Flies* is a theme Argento also revisits often. The female killer and her psychological transfer are carried over from *The Bird with the Crystal Plumage*, and several other key characters, including Roberto with his skinny frame and long hair, are quite androgynous. Argento again seems to be subverting notions of gender roles and power struggles between the sexes.

Unlike in *Cat O'Nine Tails*, where they were just alluded to, the dark recesses of incest are explored in more depth. Nina married Roberto because he physically resembles her father; hence her intention to destroy his life and ultimately cut it short. The discussion amongst several characters at a party about why Frankenstein's monster was murderous prefigures Nina's own sexual conflicts and gender crisis. She isn't comfortable in her own skin due to the fact that she was raised as a boy by her sadistic father. Encapsulating the perverse desires of many of Argento's villains, the debate of these characters, while trite, centres on homicidal impulses triggered by a frustrated libido.

God and Roberto meet up at an International Exposition of Funerary Arts during one scene. Amongst the displays of designer coffins lurks a heart-shaped one with a red velvet interior, reflecting Argento's own brand of 'eroticised' death. God dryly states, perhaps in a tongue-in-cheek aside from Argento himself, 'Death is a commercial necessity.'

As in many other Argento films, drapes often signify an entry into another world. When characters pass through drapes, usually red velvet ones, they are thrust headlong into a world of chaos and bloody death.

Music

Another melodic and tinkling score by Morricone caresses *Four Flies on Grey Velvet*. Dark and deeply haunting, the main theme ('Come un madrigale') wraps itself around the central motif of a childish and sad-sounding lullaby, resplendent with sultry, breathy female vocals and quieter moments when a simple drum beat mimics a panicked heartbeat. One of Morricone's most underrated orchestrations. Lively lounge-jazz pieces also pepper proceedings with a chic sound.

Argento had approached Deep Purple and Pink Floyd to score the film for him but they couldn't due to scheduling conflicts. Due to a rift between the two men, Morricone wouldn't score another film for Argento until *The Stendhal Syndrome*.

Trivia

Amongst the actors considered by Argento for the role of Roberto Tobias were Terence Stamp, Tom Courtenay, John Lennon, Ringo Starr, James Taylor and Michael York.

Verdict

Four Flies on Grey Velvet is a worthy successor to Argento's first two films. It further exemplifies and enhances his unique style and progressive approach to filmmaking. It exhibits typical tendencies of much of his later work: outstanding set pieces, stylish direction and a distinct lack of plot. As bleak as *Cat O'Nine Tails* and *Giallo*, it is one of his darkest and most pessimistic works to date.

Until recently, *Four Flies on Grey Velvet*, along with *Door into Darkness* and *Five Days of Milan*, was notoriously hard to find on DVD or VHS. Aside from a long-out-of-print French VHS release, there wasn't a widely distributed legitimate copy. 'Argentophiles' had to wade through statically troubled, fuzzy and non-English- subtitled versions to sneak a peek at this underrated and underexposed hidden gem. As of 2009, the film has finally been released on DVD and is now widely available.

DARKNESS & MILAN

Door into Darkness (1973)

After the success of his 'Animal' trilogy, Argento was approached by RAI TV to produce a new four-part *giallo* series for Italian television. He was initially reluctant to get involved, as he had decided that *Four Flies on Grey Velvet* was to be his last foray into the *giallo*. Argento also viewed working in television as something of a step down from his career in cinema. He soon changed his mind, however, when he was promised complete control and creative freedom. The result was a successful one and ensured that Argento would become a household name throughout Italy.

Il Vicino di casa/The Neighbour

Directed/Written by: Luigi Cozzi
Produced by: Dario Argento
Music by: Giorgio Gaslini
Cinematography: Elio Polacchi
Edited by: Amedeo Giomini & Alberto Moro
Production Designer: Dario Micheli
Cast: Aldo Reggiani (Luca), Laura Belli (Stefania), Mimmo Palmara (The Neighbour)

Synopsis

A young couple and their baby move into a new apartment, completely unaware that their upstairs neighbour is in the midst of covering up his wife's murder...

Il Tram/The Tram

Directed/Written/Produced by: Dario Argento – also credited as Sirio Bernadotte
Music by: Giorgio Gaslini
Cinematography: Elio Polacchi
Edited by: Amedeo Giomini
Production Designer: Dario Micheli
Cast: Paola Tedesco (Giulia), Enzo Cerusico (Commisario Giordani), Corrado Olmi (Officer Morini), Emilio Marchesini (Marco Roviti)

Synopsis

Through a series of re-enactments, an eccentric detective tries to solve the case of a young woman who was murdered on a busy tram with no eye-witnesses.

Testimone oculare/Eyewitness

Directed/Written/Produced by: Dario Argento
Co-directed by: Roberto Pariante
Co-written by: Luigi Cozzi
Music by: Giorgio Gaslini
Cinematography: Elio Polacchi
Edited by: Amedeo Giomini
Production Designer: Dario Micheli
Cast: Marilù Tolo (Roberta Leoni), Riccardo Salvino (Guido Leoni), Glauco Onorato (Police Inspector), Altea De Nicola (Anna)

Synopsis

A young woman believes she has witnessed a murder and alerts the authorities. When she returns to the scene of the crime, however, the body is gone and no one believes her story.

La Bambola/The Doll

Directed/Written by: Mario Foglietti
Co-written by: Marcella Elsberger
Produced by: Dario Argento
Music by: Giorgio Gaslini
Cinematography: Elio Polacchi
Edited by: Amedeo Giomini
Production Designer: Dario Micheli
Cast: Mara Venier (Daniela Moreschi), Robert Hoffman (Doctor), Erika Blanc (Elena Moreschi), Gianfranco D'Angelo (Police Commissioner), Umberto Raho (Psychiatrist)

Synopsis

A deranged patient escapes from a psychiatric hospital and begins to stalk several women.

Comments

Door into Darkness has a similar format to *Tales of the Unexpected* (1979–88) and, of course, *Alfred Hitchcock Presents* (1955), with each episode forming a self-contained mini-thriller with a twist. Argento realised that, with his name attached to the series, he could potentially receive a lot of media coverage and, when he decided to personally introduce each episode, it ensured further comparisons with Alfred Hitchcock.

With an allocated time of 14 days shooting for each episode, Argento set to work and gathered around him a small group of people he had collaborated with before and knew he could rely on.

The Neighbour: Directed by Luigi Cozzi, this episode was actually filmed second but broadcast first, as Argento believed it to be the perfect introduction to the series. Inspired by the work of crime writer Cornell Woolrich and starring Aldo Reggiani (*Cat O'Nine Tails*), it is a solid and entertaining episode and an excellent example of the mechanics of tension. While disbelief must be suspended in several scenes, the episode is taut and engrossing, particularly when the wife, bound and gagged, struggles to close and lock the door of their apartment as their neighbour makes his way back from digging shallow graves on the beach. The calm collection of the neighbour contrasted with the desperate and frenzied struggling of the couple anticipates the unrushed and purposeful movements of the likes of Michael Myers (*Halloween*) and Jason Voorhees (*Friday the 13th*, 1980), as they inexorably move in for the kill.

Argento's brief appearance at the beginning is slyly humorous as he introduces the episode by the side of a road, thumbing a lift with the couple at the centre of the story. Also amusing is when the couple sit down to watch *Abbott and Costello Meet Frankenstein* (1948), a film that showcases how horror dates so quickly, with its once-menacing monsters reduced to comedic parodies upstaged by a couple of goofy comedians.

The Tram: Based on an idea Argento had for a sequence in *The Bird with the Crystal Plumage*, this episode revolves around the murder of a young woman onboard a busy tram. The sequence was eventually dropped from *The Bird with the Crystal Plumage* and never shot, though it's easy to see why Argento wanted to return to it as it deals explicitly with one of his major preoccupations: the fallibility of the human eye and the misinterpretation of a vital clue.

Even though the murder occurs in a tram full of passengers, no one seems to notice and the detective working on the case believes he has overlooked a vital piece of evidence and becomes obsessed with solving it. Typical of Argento's work, the audience is presented with a seemingly insignificant detail that eventually becomes paramount to unlocking the secret of what actually happened.

RAI insisted the murder weapon be changed to a hook, as the initial knife was considered too phallic. There are also a few sly nods to Agatha Christie's novel *Murder on the Orient Express*.

This particular episode revels in Argento's characteristic prowling camerawork, particularly in the latter scenes where the detective's girlfriend is menaced in the deserted tram depot. The various exterior shots of the tram slinking through the city at night foreshadow the shots of the train hurtling through the dark in *Sleepless* and the automatic doors of the tram reflect the sinister qualities similar doors would take on in the opening scene of *Suspiria*.

As usual, Argento scatters a series of visual and audio clues throughout the seemingly wandering narrative, just to ensure viewers remain alert.

Perhaps highlighting his initial hesitance to become involved with the project, Argento used a directorial pseudonym on this episode, Sirio Bernadotte, as he feared the overuse of his name in the credits might undermine his reputation.

Eyewitness: Initially helmed by Roberto Pariante, Argento stepped in as director of this episode after four days of filming as he was dissatisfied with what Pariante had shot. He completed the rest of the filming himself and invited Luigi Cozzi to re-shoot Pariante's prior efforts.

This episode contains moments of lavish camerawork and Argento peppers proceedings with point-of-view shots and strange angles, alluding to the possibly unhinged mind and severe paranoia of the protagonist. One such bizarre shot would be repeated in *Suspiria*: as the camera moves slowly towards the heroine it appears to be sitting on a tray next to a drink.

The story unravels coyly and Argento creates a smothering atmosphere of claustrophobia and tension, which, by the climax, where Roberta is menaced in her shadowy house by a mysterious assailant, has become almost unbearable. Roberta was played by Argento's partner at the time, Marilù Tolo, a sultry beauty reminiscent of a young Elizabeth Taylor.

The Doll: While the final episode is perhaps the most conventional, it is interesting because of the way it gathers the various strands of Argento's career path, past and future, together. Written and directed by the co-writer of *Four Flies on Grey Velvet*, Mario Foglietti,

The Doll is pure style over substance. The simple tale of an escaped psychiatric patient stalking a series of beautiful women is enhanced by the way in which it is shot. Boasting what would become familiar imagery in Argento's later work, it features creeping camerawork, point-of-view shots and beautiful women in peril. Foglietti at times appears to be paying homage to the films of his producer, highlighting the fact that, even at this early stage in his career, Argento's style was distinctive and instantly recognisable.

Its sting-in-the-tail twist would later be repeated in the music video for The Prodigy's 'Smack My Bitch Up' (1997).

Door into Darkness was a hit and ensured Argento's status as a cultural icon in Italy; his reputation as a master of the macabre and the 'Italian Hitchcock' was sealed. Unsuspecting audiences were treated to all manner of violence and alluring carnage on what was essentially prime-time TV. Italy only had two TV channels at the time and this went some way to helping the series find success. The creative control Argento was promised didn't happen though, as RAI TV imposed several cuts, trimming a few scenes in each episode to soften the violence.

Audiences were still shocked, however, by the stylish scenes of murder and mayhem that remained after the cuts. When his name appeared above future titles, audiences would know what to expect from Dario Argento.

Le cinque giornate/The Five days of Milan (1973)

Directed/Written by: Dario Argento
Co-written by: Nanni Balestrini
Produced by: Claudio Argento
Music by: Giorgio Gaslini
Cinematography: Luigi Kuveiller
Edited by: Franco Fraticelli
Production Designer: Giuseppe Bassan

Special Effects: Aldo Gasparri
Cast: Adriano Celentano (Cainazzo), Enzo Cerusico (Marcelli), Marilù Tolo (The Countess), Glauco Onorato (Zampino), Luisa De Santis (Pregnant Woman), Carla Tatò (The Widow)

Synopsis

Milan, 1849. Freed from prison when an errant cannonball blasts a hole in the wall of his cell, petty thief Cainazzo embarks on an odyssey around Milan with his sidekick Marcelli, a local baker, in search of his former accomplice, Zampino, who owes him a share of their last heist. On their journey they encounter a nymphomaniac countess, help a pregnant woman give birth, get recruited by both sides of a burgeoning revolution and witness the streets of Milan explode with violence and bloodshed.

Background

Argento had become somewhat irked that Italian cinemas were now saturated with *giallo* pictures and, while *Four Flies on Grey Velvet* had performed well in Italy, it was poorly received in other places. After his brief, albeit successful, foray into television with *Door into Darkness*, the director thought it was time for a change in direction, and his next film served as a love letter to the Italian audiences who had embraced his work.

Distancing himself from the *gialli* glut, his next feature doesn't really sit comfortably within his oeuvre and is something of an oddity, much like Cronenberg's *Fast Company* (1979) or Wes Craven's *Music of the Heart* (1999). *The Five Days of Milan* is a dark historical comedy and was actually written before *Four Flies on Grey Velvet*. Argento revised the script with a view to producing it and arranging for Nanni Loy to direct. Loy had previously directed a number of historical dramas; however, once the cast and crew for *Five Days* had been assembled, they requested that Argento direct it, given his popularity at the time and the fact that he wrote it. Argento relented and took the helm. While his previous work had comedic aspects in the form of odd and eccentric characters, Argento had never attempted outright comedy before. The results are uneven as he amalgamates coarse humour, slapstick and extreme violence.

Comments

Five Days has been described by Argento as a purely Italian film for an Italian audience: it was never released outside of Italy. An allegorical film, its portrayal of a city in tumult not only depicts the Italian revolution of 1848, but also reflects the 1968 student riots in Paris. This theme would be revisited again by Argento's friend Bertolucci, in his film *The Dreamers* (2005).

Five Days marked several firsts for Argento; not only was it his first foray outside of the *giallo*, but it also marked the first time he would work with his brother Claudio, who produced the film. It would be the beginning of a rocky but ultimately rewarding collaboration. Claudio produced all of his brother's films until *Tenebrae*, when they fell out because of Claudio's desire to produce films away from Dario. Amongst other films he produced was Alejandro Jodorowsky's *Santa Sangre* (1989), a deeply disturbing and hauntingly beautiful film that could arguably be described as 'Argentoesque'. The brothers reconciled their differences several years later after the death of their father, and *Two Evil Eyes* marked Claudio's return to producing his brother's work.

Unfortunately, *Five Days* was a commercial and critical failure, dubbed an awkward film by critics who didn't appreciate Argento's blend of comedy and cynical politics. The juvenile humour that proved so unpopular is especially evident in a scene where Cainazzo, on his way to the headquarters of the revolutionaries, carries an Italian flag to blend in. He is oblivious of the small army of followers who subsequently gather behind him, wrongly thinking he is patriotically leading them to battle. Every time he stops, they stop. The action is speeded up, adding to the 'hilarity'. The scene in which Cainazzo and Marcelli are recruited to help a pregnant woman deliver her baby is especially doused in slapstick and Laurel-and-Hardy-style shenanigans.

Argento's problems with Tony Musante on *The Bird with the Crystal Plumage* would be resurrected in the form of his new leading man, Italian pop singer Adriano Celentano, who was rather demanding and domineering on the set.

Style/technique

Under the guidance of Argento, Kuveiller gave *Five Days* a distinct style and look, similar to that of a typical Spaghetti Western. The director excels in perfecting his experimental camera movements and compositions. The film contains many tracking shots and an overabundance of stylisation: slow-motion battle scenes, prowling camerawork, indulgent editing, bloody special effects and a bizarre soundtrack.

There is one scene that could stylistically fit into any of Argento's other films. The scene features the Countess, a raging nymphomaniac, played by Argento's lover at the time, Marilù Tolo, wandering through the halls of her grand house, torn drapes billowing around her, glancing back longingly as the camera, in stalker mode, glides ominously along after her. This is blatant Argento imagery; however, after it is revealed that the Countess is luring the men who defended her house into her bedroom to thank them by sexually pleasuring them, we are back in the realm of bizarre comedy. The audacity of this scene may achieve a few gasps of exasperation from the audience, as the Countess reveals her selfless intentions by flashing the crowd of men her thigh as they jostle to get to her.

Another scene mirroring more familiar Argento territory occurs when Cainazzo arrives at the headquarters on Vige Street, looking for his elusive friend Zampino. The camera ceaselessly follows him around the courtyard, up the winding stairs and along the corridors of the ornate building until he comes to a stop outside the boardroom of the public officials. Cue more juvenile comedy and the strange shot of a man yelling insults out of the window, only for the camera to whip across the landscape and seemingly deliver this barrage of expletives to the King in Rome.

With this vivaciousness Argento was clearly paving the way for his next film, *Deep Red*, where he and Luigi Kuveiller would fully realise their artistic talents to create a stunning masterpiece.

Themes

While *The Five Days of Milan* is distinctly unlike Argento's other work, it does contain a number of familiar motifs and themes.

Like many of the maestro's protagonists, Cainazzo is ejected, purely by chance, into a world in chaos. Freed from prison by a wayward cannonball, he wanders into the city to find it on the brink of revolution and becomes unintentionally mixed up in events.

The violence in this film, while still lavish and stylised, is markedly different from that depicted in Argento's other films. As the author of *Art of Darkness*, Chris Gallant, points out: 'The brutality is frequently more harsh, more abrasive and impersonal than the intimacy of murder – that which exists between Argento's killers and their victims.'[10]

There are, of course, many shots of knives penetrating vulnerable bodies in *Five Days*, but as they occur in the context of large battle scenes they lack any sort of impact.

One slow-motion shot of a dying mother with her distraught infant crawling from her embrace to wander into the rioting crowd is quite affecting and is accompanied by the desperately moving strains of *Ave Maria*.

Though she appeared in the *Door into Darkness* episode *Eyewitness*, the casting of Marilù Tolo in *Five Days* marked the first time that one of Argento's lovers had been featured in one of his films.

This would be echoed to much darker effect with Daria Nicolodi and all of her subsequent roles in Argento's work. As mentioned, certain critics have suggested that the disintegration of the relationship between Argento and Nicolodi can be charted through the course of the films they made together.

Music

The soundtrack of *The Five Days of Milan* is as uneven as Argento's attempts at comedy. Alongside subtle orchestral arrangements, Gaslini also utilises inappropriate piano compositions that are reminiscent of those that accompanied Charlie Chaplin's silent antics. He also incorporates synthesised remixes of various classical pieces, echoing Wendy Carlos' work on *A Clockwork Orange* (1971), to humorous but ultimately dire effect.

Trivia

Marilù Tolo was offered the part of Ursa in *Superman II* (1980) before it went to Sarah Douglas.

Verdict

While nowhere near as bad as *Phantom of the Opera*, this still marks a decidedly low point in Argento's career. Luckily, the director realised that his strengths did not lie in this sort of haphazard malarkey and he really proved what he was capable of with his next film.

BLOOD RUNS DEEP

Profondo Rosso/Deep Red (1975)

Directed/Written by: Dario Argento
Co-written by: Bernardino Zapponi
Produced by: Claudio Argento
Music by: Goblin & Giorgio Gaslini
Cinematography: Luigi Kuveiller
Edited by: Franco Fraticelli
Art Director: Giuseppe Bassan
Special Effects: Germano Natali & Carlo Rambaldi
Cast: David Hemmings (Marc Daly), Daria Nicolodi (Gianna Brezzi), Gabriele Lavia (Carlo), Macha Méril (Helga Ulmann), Giuliana Calandra (Amanda Righetti), Glauco Mauri (Professor Giordani), Clara Calamai (Marta)
Also known as: *The Hatchet Murders*, *The Deep Red Hatchet Murders*

Synopsis

After sensing the presence of a killer during a séance, psychic Helga Ulmann is brutally murdered by an unseen assailant. English jazz musician Marc Daly witnesses the murder. He believes he saw something strange at the scene of the crime that could help unveil the killer, but can't remember exactly what it was. He teams up with feisty reporter Gianna and their investigation triggers another spate of murders.

The victims all share a connection with a mysterious villa. Marc and Gianna must evade attempts on their own lives as they get closer to exhuming a dark secret that someone is intent on keeping buried – at any cost.

Background

Argento dreamt up the story for *Deep Red* while staying at his father's old house in the countryside, in a state of solitary exile. He wrote the majority of the screenplay there too, giving himself nightmares and a few sleepless nights. Returning to civilisation, he soon finished the script with Fellini collaborator Bernardino Zapponi. The rich and full-bodied *Deep Red* is often described as Argento's masterpiece and a major defining moment in the history of *gialli*.

Filmed in Turin, the shoot took 16 weeks, beginning in September 1974. According to Argento, this was a fitting locale as it is home to the largest number of practising Satanists in Europe. He would later return to Turin's bewitching streets to film *Sleepless* in 2001 and *Giallo* in 2008.

Comments

During the course of his career thus far, Argento had established himself as a master of the *giallo* and obviously had a flair for creating lush scenes of terror and suspense. After his brief and ill-advised venture outside of the *giallo* with *Five Days of Milan*, the director returned to the genre that made his name with a vengeance, presenting to the world his blood-soaked and harrowing opus.

Deep Red essentially blew imitators out of the way when it was released in 1975 to unsuspecting audiences.

The film is also significant in that it marked the first time Argento worked with his future partner and muse, Daria Nicolodi. Her role in front of and behind Argento's camera was pivotal in shaping the director's future career trajectory. She appears alongside David Hemmings and the two display a remarkable chemistry not replicated between two leads in an Argento film until *The Card Player*.

Amongst the startling and luridly depicted murders, and the general perversity on display, *Deep Red* is also a very humorous film. The comic banter between the two leads often provides light relief, without detracting from Argento's carefully built-up atmosphere of foreboding and dread. Adding to the creepiness on display is the fact that much of the film takes place at night, in the oddly deserted streets of the city. Events unfold in an almost dreamlike narrative, similar to that of Jacques Tourneur's *The Leopard Man* (1943), a film Argento references in *Four Flies on Grey Velvet*, with its bizarre logic and stand-out set pieces. As with Tourneur's film, we are usually only introduced to characters just as they are about to be murdered.

Deep Red was a huge influence on John Carpenter and he directed *Halloween* (1978) in homage to this movie. Argento's use of widescreen persistently suggests that someone or something could be lurking in the corner of the screen, ever ready to pounce. This was echoed by Carpenter, who also borrowed the idea of a woman alone in her house with a killer moving into frame behind her and her subsequent attempts to defend herself with a knitting needle from *Deep Red*. The demise of this victim, author Amanda Righetti, is also referenced in *Halloween II* (1981) in the scene where Nurse Karen is murdered in a hot tub. Argento's groundbreaking camerawork further inspired Carpenter in the creepy opening shots of *Halloween*, where we witness proceedings from the killer's point of view. *Deep Red* also features a killer brandishing a kitchen knife, as did *Halloween*, and all that particular implement's associations with domesticity and familial trimmings are subverted in the film's revelation.

Argento has on a number of occasions stated that he likes to confine displays of violence and inflictions of pain to common experiences, so that viewers are able to empathise to some extent with the pain suffered. His victims are often cut, as in the case with psychic Helga being shoved through a pane of glass, and her colleague having his teeth knocked out before being stabbed. Extreme as these scenarios are, Argento utilises them for the very reason that we have all, at one time or another, scalded or cut ourselves, or banged a tooth on a glass.

Like the majority of Argento's work, *Deep Red* did not escape the omniscient gaze of the censor, and heavy cuts were imposed on the film outside of Italy, notably a couple of shots involving cruelty to animals: two dogs fighting and an impaled lizard, Argento's favourite animal. In America, essential expository scenes that gracefully layer the film with subtext were excised and the violence was also trimmed.

Style/Technical

Deep Red features an extravagant and baroque look that naturally paves the way for the more majestic and surreal leanings of *Suspiria* and *Inferno*. The composition, framing and colour palette were groundbreaking. Sets and lighting rear up of their own accord as though they were also characters in the film. Argento's dazzlingly mobile camera rarely pauses to catch its breath, or allow the viewer to catch theirs, revelling in several beautifully choreographed and vivid death scenes.

The camera often acts as though it has a mind of its own: when not presenting events from the killers' or victims' perspectives, or offering a detached view of proceedings, it wanders off, unmotivated by the actions of any of the characters. The result is strangely disorientating as the viewer struggles to decipher whose point of view we are experiencing, before realising that it is none but that of the impartial lens. At one point it even breaks away from two characters walking down the street to watch some television in a nearby house.

Deep Red is a film of constant interruptions. Not only are various characters disturbed in their daily routines by the psychotic killer, but even the opening titles aren't safe as they are abruptly stalled to reveal the mysterious and tantalising opening murder. In later scenes, Marc interrupts his band while they are rehearsing to tell them to loosen up and improvise. Argento seems to be constantly prodding his audience with these disruptions to remind them to be attentive and keep a close watch on proceedings, where anything can happen.

Themes

Sigmund Freud stated that 'Repression operates upon memories that are traumatic or upon memories that are associated with traumatic experience'.

Deep Red, Argento's darkly extravagant tale of repressed trauma and mariticide, marks the return of a simmering Freudian subtext to the director's work. The traumatic event of the youngster witnessing a murder, depicted in the flashback during the opening credits, is presented to the audience as a repressed memory, surfacing to haunt an as yet unidentified character. No Argento film is seemingly complete without a killer obsessed with a past crime they will do anything to conceal! While Argento subverts many of the clichés of the subgenre, with *Deep Red* he has simultaneously created the perfect embodiment of all that the *giallo* is.

Once again, the themes of voyeurism and spectatorship are abundant and executed with exact precision. The camera reprises its role as killer and stalker, maiming its victims in glorious close-up. Weird perspective shots draw our gaze to specific objects and situations, tantalising us with possible clues. The gaze of the audience is quite often deliberately misdirected too, as in the scene where Marc goes to the psychic's apartment to try to help her. The composition of the shot draws our gaze to the end of the hallway, whereas something very significant is actually occurring halfway down the hall.

Marc Daly is the quintessential Argento protagonist, an 'outsider' living abroad. Marc assumes the responsibility of detective and any encounters with the police seem to indicate that they are as ineffectual as most cops in Argento films. Constantly eating and blustering around, their voracious appetites recall the food-obsessed cop in *Cat O'Nine Tails*.

Hemmings plays the character with a light-hearted touch, high-lighting situations in which he is emasculated by his beautiful sidekick Gianna. He loses several arm-wrestling fights with her, is rescued by her from a burning building and suffers the humiliation dealt out by her dodgy car seat. Marc is constantly stripped of his masculine pride in typical Argento fashion. Their relationship, like that of Giordani and Arno in *Cat O'Nine Tails* is warm and platonic; unconventionally, it never becomes romantic.

This heralds the beginning of a series of consecutive films made by the director, with the exception of *Inferno*, that would feature strong female characters at the centre of dark events. Even though Gianna is essentially a sidekick, she has a stronger presence than any of Argento's previous female characters and easily paves the way for the likes of Suzy in *Suspiria*, Jennifer in *Phenomena*, Betty in *Opera*, Aura in *Trauma*, Anna in *The Card Player*, Sara in *Mother of Tears* and Linda and Celine in *Giallo*. Nicolodi plays Gianna as a fast-talking, ball-busting reporter akin to Rosalind Russell in *His Girl Friday* (1940).

Eyes also feature heavily throughout the film's striking array of imagery. Extreme close-ups reveal the killer donning dark eyeliner in an almost ritualistic manner, conveying primal rage and dark aggression.

As critic Julian Grainger comments in *Art of Darkness*: 'Murder as sex and spying as foreplay in *Deep Red*. The act of watching is far from neutral.'[11] Seeing events from their privileged position, the viewer is often implicated in the perverse goings-on. This is most notable during the murder of the writer; as she is beaten she looks directly into the camera with a look of helpless desperation, a motif Argento toyed with in *The Bird with the Crystal Plumage*, *Cat O'Nine Tails* and *Tenebrae*. As in the 'Animal' trilogy, the protagonist sees and misinterprets crucial events, and spends the remainder of the film trying to remember and reinterpret what they saw. Marc witnesses the gory demise of the psychic and spends the rest of the film trying to remember a detail at the crime scene, striving to find a solution to the puzzle. His viewpoint is constantly reshaped as the twisted logic of the narrative unfolds. The premise of a clue being buried in someone's mind, and their attempting to recall it, is reminiscent of Hitchcock's *Spellbound* (1945). It is cruelly ironic that the psychic's power is the reason for her murder, also the very thing that could have perhaps saved her, an idea further explored in *Phenomena*.

Argento does his best to conceal the identity of the fiendish murderer; vigilant audiences will be rewarded with various clues throughout, as well as enough red herrings to shake a large knife at. Again with Argento, it is the journey and not the destination that is important.

Art is once again presented as possessing sinister and insidious qualities. When the killer is reflected in a mirror, her features are hidden from Marc by a grotesque 'Munchian' painting of contorted faces. He assumes her face to be part of the canvas. A child's drawing also reveals an important clue to the killer's identity. Argento playfully recreates scenes from famous paintings; the very last shot of Marc staring into the red depths of a pool of blood mirrors the actions in Caravaggio's 'Narcissus'. The emphasis of the gaze is reiterated here and in the scene outside the bar where Carlo hangs out, echoing Hopper's 'Nighthawks'.

The killer in *Deep Red*, as in *The Bird with the Crystal Plumage*, *Four Flies on Grey Velvet*, *Tenebrae*, *Phenomena*, *Opera*, *Trauma* and *Sleepless*, is dressed in the traditional *giallo* villain garb of dark raincoat and black leather gloves. Leather features prominently in these killers' wardrobes, and the air hangs heavy with connotations of fetishism.

Gender and notions of family are again toyed with, as the film's killer is revealed to be a middle-aged woman whose son, Carlo, describes himself as having 'strange sexual tastes' and is having relations with a transvestite. Argento cast a woman as Carlo's male, cross-dressing lover Massimo, an interesting choice that is revisited in *Tenebrae*, where a transsexual actor portrays the role of the woman in the Freudian flashbacks.

The idea of a monstrous and dominant mother is another recurring theme of Argento's; one only has to view the 'Three Mothers' trilogy, *Opera*, *Phenomena*, *Trauma*, *The Stendhal Syndrome* and *Giallo* to confirm this.

Disturbingly, a strong connection between death and childhood exists in the film. A child witnesses the savage murder of his father in the flashback and the film is laced with shots of children's toys. Is this child the murderer? The caretaker of the 'haunted' villa has a morbid and cruel daughter whom he describes as inherently evil. There is also the significance of the children's lullaby, heard every time the killer strikes, echoing a twisted and chilling link to childhood, where traumatic events can corrupt innocence and bloom into psychosis.

The 'haunted' villa, referred to in the film as 'The House of the Screaming Boy' (a fitting title for any *giallo*!), brings to mind the damned houses harbouring dreadful and filthy secrets in the 'Three Mothers' trilogy and in Soavi's films *The Church* and *The Sect*, which Argento co-wrote and produced. Home might be where the heart is, but in an Argento movie the heart has been ripped out and repeatedly stabbed.

Drapes signifying our entry into another world again feature heavily in *Deep Red*; we are ushered into a theatre where a lecture on parapsychology is taking place through heavy red velvet curtains.

Music

Argento once again approached Pink Floyd to score one of his pictures, as he had with *Four Flies on Grey Velvet*, and once again they had to turn him down. Giorgio Gaslini, composer of the scores for *Five Days of Milan* and *Door into Darkness*, wrote and recorded some music for *Deep Red* but Argento wasn't completely satisfied with it, feeling it wasn't as progressive as the film. Having been introduced to the music of Goblin, Argento approached the classically trained progressive-rock band and they accepted his offer with gusto. The throbbing score the band provided marked the beginning of a stunning collaboration between Argento and Goblin founder Claudio Simonetti that has lasted many years.

Deep Red's bass-heavy, punk-Gothic score drives home the ferocity of the imagery on display and the intensity of the acts of violence. Jangling and pulsating, it weaves together a combination of prog-rock and jazz to distinctive and highly stylish effect. The pounding piano riff, which would offer yet more inspiration to John Carpenter, is hypnotic in its simplicity and repetitive rhythm.

A few of Gaslini's efforts still remain in the film, light jazzy pieces more reminiscent of Morricone's melodic compositions. Gaslini also wrote the eerie lullaby that is integral to the plot.

Verdict

Deep Red is a stunning and uncompromising film that epitomises Argento's work. Shocking violence, ravishing camerawork, hallucinatory score and gallons of blood: while this could be the description of any Argento movie, *Deep Red* truly marks the beginning of all the things Argento is revered for, and really stands out as one of the director's most evocative and chilling films. A macabre masterpiece.

ITALIAN GOTHIC

Suspiria (1977)

'Do you know anything about witches?'

Directed/Written by: Dario Argento (also music collaborator)
Co-written by: Daria Nicolodi
Produced by: Claudio Argento
Music by: Goblin
Cinematography: Luciano Tovoli
Edited by: Franco Fraticelli
Production Designer: Giuseppe Bassan
Special Effects: Germano Natali
Cast: Jessica Harper (Suzy Banyon), Stefania Casini (Sara), Joan Bennett (Madame Blanc), Alida Valli (Miss Tanner), Eva Axén (Pat Hingle), Flavio Bucci (Daniel), Udo Kier (Doctor Frank Mandel)

Synopsis

American ballet student Suzy Banyon enrols at a prestigious dance academy in Freiberg, Germany. Her arrival coincides with a raging storm and the savage murder of another student at the demonic hands of an unseen attacker. A number of odd occurrences and other grisly deaths suggest that there is something rotten lurking within the heart of the school and Suzy begins to suspect that it is actually a witches' coven, determined to unleash untold ills upon an unsuspecting world.

Background

After the success of *Deep Red*, Argento wanted to attempt something just as different from his previous work as *Deep Red* had been. *Suspiria* was Argento's second foray outside of the *giallo* and in it he strays into full-blown supernatural-horror territory, creating a nightmarish and truly unforgettable world.

It serves as the introduction to the sinister figures of the Three Mothers, three powerful and evil witches who unleash suffering and misery on all who encounter them. The wrath of Mater Suspiriorum (Mother of Sighs) is encountered in *Suspiria*, while *Inferno* and *Mother of Tears* showcase the wickedness of Mater Tenebrarum (Mother of Darkness) and Mater Lachrymarum (Mother of Tears) respectively.

Keen to embark on a story that had a self-contained mythology, Argento had considered adapting several of HP Lovecraft's chilling narratives for the screen, but decided that transferring those cosmic tales of horror and madness from page to film would not have done them justice.

Argento was inspired by a number of sources when developing *Suspiria*. One was the vivid, drug-induced writing of Thomas De Quincey, particularly his work *Suspiria de Profundis* (*Sighs from the Depths*), with its dark depictions of Levana and Our Ladies of Sorrow forming the basis for the Three Mothers. Something of an unholy trinity, the Three Mothers are aligned with the three graces, three fates, three muses and three furies in De Quincey's opium-fuelled and feverish scribblings.

Lewis Carroll and the Brothers Grimm seem to have had an additional effect on Argento, as *Suspiria* unravels before us like a morbid and fascinating fairytale, thrusting the viewer into a nightmarish and delirious looking-glass.

This was also the first time that Argento drew on the obvious influence of Edgar Allan Poe, in a garish tale of the occult, the supernatural and its macabre intrusions on a seemingly normal situation.

Argento co-wrote the screenplay with Daria Nicolodi, who relayed tales told by her grandmother, who had spent time in finishing school where black magic was practised in the dead of night by both teachers and pupils.

As Nicolodi was unable to appear in the film due to an injury, Argento offered the roles of Suzy and Sara, two roles she had been tipped to play, to other actresses. Nicolodi can still be seen in a brief shot in the airport at the beginning of the film, walking past Suzy towards the exit.

Despite its worldwide success, *Suspiria*'s distributor Fox was somewhat embarrassed by the film and, rather than release it under their own banner, they used a subsidiary corporation called International Classics Inc.

Comments

Structured much like the narrative of a fairytale, the story begins with a brief introduction to our heroine Suzy Banyon, a stranger in a foreign land, by way of a 'once upon a time'-style narration.

Suspiria is considered Argento's biggest success, the blood-red jewel in a crown already saturated in sparkling claret. Before *Suspiria*, Argento had always been adventurous and experimental, and he would continue this approach to filmmaking after *Suspiria* too; but each subsequent offering has always been compared to this film, with fans and critics declaring it the peak of Argento's career.

Jessica Harper, whom Argento had seen in Brian De Palma's *Phantom of the Paradise* (1974), has the ability to combine innocence and naivety with a strong will and level head, making her the perfect choice to play Suzy, one of Argento's many strong female protagonists. Harper was eager to work with Argento in Italy as she was a fan of his previous films. Udo Kier portrays Frank Mandel, a psychiatrist Suzy approaches for help. Kier's English at the time wasn't strong and he had to be prompted from behind the camera.

As all of Argento's films prior to *Two Evil Eyes* had been filmed without sound, this wasn't too big an obstacle for the actor to overcome. Argento cast Alida Valli in the role of the domineering Miss Tanner and Joan Bennett as Madame Blanc. Valli previously starred in the darkly poetic *Eyes Without A Face* (1960) and was the widow of Fritz Lang, whom Argento greatly admired. Her and Bennett's characters are like the archetypal 'ugly sisters', distributing torment and cruelty to the young beauties. Madame Blanc, with her layered-on make-up and fading beauty, resembles Bette Davis in *Whatever Happened to Baby Jane?* (1962).

Style/Technical

Suspiria is a visceral onslaught of vision and colour. Argento bombards the viewer with lurid colours and renders them breathless with his opulent set design, sado-erotic imagery and extremely sinister and powerful soundtrack. This sensory excess defies the belief that horror emerges from nuance and shadowy suggestion. Nothing is left to the imagination in this film.

Argento was visually inspired by Disney's *Snow White and the Seven Dwarves* (1937), with its rich, primary colour-based palette. Swirling psychedelically throughout the film is a strong, almost maniacal colour code of reds, blues and greens, evident in the lighting and baroque set design. The result is a purposefully delirious atmosphere that is both claustrophobic and utterly hellish.

Suspiria's unique look was made possible by cinematographer Luciano Tovoli, who would later lens *Tenebrae* and *Single White Female* (1992). Argento wanted the film to look anything but normal, and both he and Tovoli were interested in experimenting with lighting and shadows. Frames made of velour and tissue were utilised in capturing *Suspiria*'s lurid glow. Arc lights, mirrors and close-up shots helped to manipulate light in a way that standard gel frames could not. This film would also be the last ever to be 'dio-transferred': the negative was given to Technicolor who split it into three separate black-and-white negatives – one for red, one for blue and one for green. These were then printed one on top of the other to create the vibrant look of the finished film. Argento insisted that Technicolor also use the highest possible contrast to increase the presence of primary colours.

Argento's camera is as restless as ever and performs some startling and meticulously planned moves in *Suspiria*, most notably in the scene depicting the blind pianist's demise in a deserted city square. It is worth mentioning that the square used in this scene was Munich Square, from which the Third Reich was administered during World War II. Is this perhaps Argento aligning the evil and oppression of the Three Mothers with that of the Nazis?

Watching and stalking the pianist from the roof of a vast building, the camera swoops down over his head as though on the wings of some terrible demon. The camera was attached to a cable, and when it slid down to a certain point, a mechanism on the cable was released, forcing the camera to lift up and over the actor's head.

In another scene where Suzy drives back through the forest, she sees Pat running through the trees in the distance, her red cape fluttering behind her in the storm. Argento films the girl between the trees from the moving taxi and, as she runs, the result is like a zoetrope illusion, enhancing the childish nature of the characters, while remaining sinister and dripping with dark fairytale connotations. These grandiose, almost self-conscious flourishes keep the viewer on their toes and perpetually command attention.

Argento also draws influence from the Expressionism of the set design in such films as Robert Wiene's *The Cabinet of Dr Caligari* (1920), FW Murnau's *Nosferatu: A Symphony of Horror* (1922) and Fritz Lang's *Metropolis* (1927), all of which featured nightmarish production design that dwarfed the actors and imposed itself on the film, essentially a character in its own right. Argento's use of lighting and dreamlike plot structure also recalls Carl Theodor Dreyer's

Vampyr (1932), a stylistic and abstract film containing a loose story linked together by powerful and darkly beautiful images. The stylised and angular high Gothicism evident in the sets of *Suspiria* is no less drenched in Expressionism. The 'Escher-esque' designs on the walls of Pat's friend's flat flood the screen, practically devour the characters, and defy logic as much as the film itself. The flat is also situated in the most elaborate and imposing building imaginable – another perfect example of how the sets dwarf the action.

It is also interesting to note that the name of the building in which the dance academy is based translates as 'House of the Whale'. It almost seems to have a life of its own and literally swallows up all those who enter it. This concept of a 'living' house is repeated in *Inferno*, with its deranged architect Varelli actually stating that the house has become his body. The idea of something rotting and corrupt lurking in the heart of such a building is creepily conveyed by maggots raining from the ceiling onto the heads of the unsuspecting students.

The lighting of the film seems to create shadows more than dispel them. As the camera hovers outside the window in the blackness of the night, spying on Pat from afar, the light from the room is the only light in a space of complete darkness, emphasising Pat's isolation and vulnerability. This notion of a fragile light keeping the dark tentatively at bay is echoed in a close-up shot of a light bulb in Suzy's room, its coil dimming slowly when switched off, engulfing the room in darkness. Contrasts of light and dark are used to similar and startling effect in the scene where Suzy is struck down with illness in a long hallway after an ogre-like maid shines the light from a crystal she is polishing in Suzy's face. The whole hallway is lit up instantly in an ethereal light, the dust visibly dancing through the air like a brief and intimate cosmos, as Suzy swoons and stumbles like a dying swan.

The editing also goes some way to disorienting the viewer, rendering everyday objects and situations as moments of abject terror, with sudden changes of viewpoint and jump cuts from extreme close-ups to wider shots. This is highlighted in the scene where Suzy and Sara tread water in the spooky swimming pool as we watch them from above. Is this just Argento showing off, or are we seeing them from some hideous entity's viewpoint?

Argento also craftily references the ink-blots of Rorschach in a shot featuring the aftermath of the opening double murder. The exquisite corpses are arranged rather like a morbid art installation, with various splotches of bright-red blood dabbled and pooling around them.

Themes

The most obvious recurring theme here is that of the monstrous maternal figure, carrying on from Carlo's deranged mother in *Deep Red* and preceding the delirious antics of abominable mothers in *Inferno*, *Phenomena*, *Opera*, *Trauma*, *Mother of Tears* and *Giallo*.

A 'House of the Damned' lies at the dark heart of *Suspiria*, and the unspeakable acts of evil hidden within its walls recall the 'House of the Screaming Boy' in *Deep Red*. They also feature prominently in *Inferno* and are referenced again in *Mother of Tears*.

While much of Argento's past work has distinct Freudian undertones, *Suspiria* features typically Jungian imagery of fire and water. Jung's writing emphasised the importance of dreams in psychoanalysis, and Argento has on a number of occasions stated that his films have been inspired by the ideas of this philosopher.

Psychological transfer and repressed memories leading to psychotic breakdowns are commonplace in Argento's films. In *Suspiria*, this theme is reiterated in Suzy's conversations with Frank Mandel, as he suggests that notions of witchcraft, superstition and devilry are linked to mental disorders: 'Broken minds, not broken mirrors.'

Argento initially wanted the students to be young girls portrayed by actresses between the ages of 12 and 14, but this idea was quashed by his father who said it would be too controversial and might risk the film being banned outright. However, the story is still told as though from a young girl's perspective. Suzy is innocent

Dario Argento

and naïve and her classmates immature and petty; her teachers are overbearing and unreasonable. The actors are dwarfed by the grand set designs and, as a result, look infinitely smaller. Interestingly, all of the door handles featured in the school are placed quite high up, giving the impression that the girls are childlike in stature. Pat's distorted features pressed tight against the window are reminiscent of a naughty and childish game, until her face is pushed completely through the glass by her ghastly attacker.

A sort of dream logic eventually intrudes and overpowers what little logic was contained in the plot to begin with, forcing the viewer on a journey into nightmarish realms where anything is possible and no one is safe.

Like previous Argento protagonists, Suzy notices a clue at the beginning of the film that doesn't make any sense to her. She spends the rest of the film trying to identify the significance of something she heard Pat scream as she left the school in the thunderstorm raging when Suzy arrived. The tantalisingly cryptic clue was revealed with the uttering of the words 'secret' and 'irises'. Eagle-eyed viewers may see what Pat was referring to in several scenes set in Madame Blanc's office.

Habitually pushing the boundaries of onscreen violence, Argento, outdoing himself yet again, wanted to begin *Suspiria* in the manner in which most horror films end – with breathtakingly climactic, almost cathartic scenes of devastating violence. *Suspiria* contains a number of murders that must surely be amongst the most nasty and cruel in the history of horror cinema. The opening double murder is intensely graphic and unflinching in its depiction of savage death at the hands of an unseen, presumably supernatural assailant. As a result, the audience are left to worry about what could possibly come next in a film with such a blood-soaked, bravura opening.

Argento cheekily references his directorial debut, *The Bird with the Crystal Plumage*, in *Suspiria*'s closing scenes. Suzy, upon entering the lair of the Black Witch, Helena Marcos (Mother of Sighs), sees an ornamental crystal bird and uses one of its glass feathers to stab Helena in the neck. This also provides another instance in Argento's oeuvre when art is used to deadly effect.

Drapes and doorways as thresholds to otherworldly places are rife throughout *Suspiria*, most notably in the opening scenes when Suzy arrives at the airport. Never before has an automatic door seemed so threatening. This visually echoes Sam's predicament involving glass doors in *The Bird with the Crystal Plumage* and highlights the thin line separating order from absolute chaos. Curtains and drapes constantly flutter in an eerie breeze, and the discovery of a secret door in Madame Blanc's office leads Suzy to the dark heart of the school where its filthy secrets are finally revealed.

Music

The score is of the utmost importance in *Suspiria*, complementing the excessive visual bombardment and driving the story forward mercilessly.

The script is admittedly sparse as Argento conveys everything through the use of visuals and music. Eerie winds, the battering of metallic drums and the shrieking of scraped strings build to an unbearable climax before settling into the sinister tinkling of a music-box lullaby over the opening credits. Strains of an Eastern European gypsy variety, both mysterious and otherworldly, become apparent. Ever present is a resonant and droning bass beat, teased along by rasping and guttural banshee wailings and whisperings, hinting inaudibly at the primal atrocities to come. The discordant guitar strumming and wizened synthesisers mark a repetitive rhythm that eventually reaches hysterical proportions – and this was to have no small influence on the work of John Carpenter. A rough cut of the soundtrack was allegedly played full blast on the set to unnerve the actors and get them into the appropriate mood.

Trivia

During Suzy's nightmarishly psychedelic taxi ride from the airport to the academy, sharp-eyed viewers will notice the almost subliminal image of a face contorted in a scream, reflected in the glass partition behind the driver when the lightning flashes. This face belongs to none other than Dario Argento himself.

Verdict

From its creepy opening scenes in the airport and the storm, to the jaw-dropping shocks of the first murders, to the point where Suzy comes face to face with her nemesis, *Suspiria* plunges the viewer into an inescapable nightmare. The intrusive soundtrack and inimitable imagery, bathed in livid reds and blues, is truly spellbinding and relentless and unlike anything before or since. Another masterpiece from Argento and one of horror cinema's greatest works.

Inferno (1980)

Directed/Written by: Dario Argento
Produced by: Claudio Argento
Music by: Keith Emerson
Cinematography: Romano Albani
Edited by: Franco Fraticelli
Art Director: Giuseppe Bassan
Special Effects: Mario Bava & Pino Leoni
Cast: Leigh McCloskey (Mark Elliot), Irene Miracle (Rose Elliot), Eleonora Giorgi (Sara), Daria Nicolodi (Countess Elise Delon Van Adler), Sacha Pitoeff (Mr Kazanian), Alida Valli (Carol), Veronica Lazar (Varelli's Nurse)

Synopsis

Rose Elliot, a writer living in New York, discovers a book written by an old alchemist named Varelli. In it he describes how he designed and built three dwelling places for three powerful witches known as the Three Mothers. Rose suspects that the building she lives in is one of these houses. She writes a letter to her brother Mark, a music student living in Rome, asking for his help, as she feels her discovery has placed her in danger from unknown forces. Before Mark arrives in New York, Rose is brutally killed by an unseen assailant. Her brother must piece together several cryptic clues in order to find out what happened to her and escape with his own life intact as the Mother of Darkness closes in.

Background

Argento's American distributors were keen for him to repeat the success of *Suspiria*. While he was waiting for George Romero to finish up *Dawn of the Dead*, Argento stayed in New York in a hotel overlooking Central Park. It was a bad winter and Argento was quite ill with hepatitis. His only correspondence with loved ones back in Italy was via the letters he wrote.

Filming of *Inferno* began in May 1979 in Rome and New York, and although it only took 14 weeks to film, due to managerial changes at Fox, who had acquired the film for distribution, all work commissioned by the previous head of production was shelved. *Inferno* was one of these unfortunate projects.

The bureaucracy Argento came up against during the making of this film was stifling to say the least and, amongst other things, he faced pressure when it came to casting. Holding true to his vision, though, Argento assembled a cast he felt satisfied with, including Irene Miracle, a friend of Bernardo Bertolucci and star of Italian horror flick *Late Night Trains* (1975), Leigh McCloskey, star of TV's *Dallas* (though James Woods was allegedly tipped to play Mark) and Italian stalwarts Veronica Lazar and Alida Valli. Argento was apparently inspired by *Last Year in Marienbad*'s (1961) dream-logic and surrealism, and the casting of Sacha Pitoeff would certainly indicate a nod to that film.

Behind the scenes, working as a production assistant, was future director of *Maniac* (1980) and *Maniac Cop* (1988) William Lustig. Lustig actually told Argento about his script for *Maniac* (a film inspired by Argento's own work and laced with depraved scenes of sex and violence) and the director was so impressed that he agreed to distribute the film in Europe. These plans fell through, however. Nicolodi was also offered a role in *Maniac* and, rather diplomatically, declined.

Comments

Argento has commented on *Inferno*, calling it his 'most sincere' and 'purest' work. A sequel to *Suspiria* and a further instalment in the ongoing sadistic saga of the Three Mothers, he had wanted *Inferno* to look and feel completely different from *Suspiria*. In the former film, we are introduced to the idea of three powerful witches; in *Inferno* we are given more information about them. We discover that they reside in three different houses around the world, one in Freiburg (as featured in *Suspiria*), one in New York (*Inferno*) and another in Rome (*Mother of Tears*).

As Rose reads from a book written by the architect and alchemist Varelli, who designed their houses, we learn more about the Three Mothers. We are told that there are three keys to unlocking the secrets of the Mothers: the first clue stipulates that the immediate environments surrounding their houses are plague ridden and omit a strange odour (Rose and Sara comment on a bitter-sweet smell in *Inferno* and the house in *Suspiria* is infested with maggots); the second key is hidden in the cellar and takes the form of a picture of one of the Three Mothers, bearing the name of whichever Mother resides in that house (Rose discovers this in the underwater ballroom); the third key is most cryptic of all and the book simply states that it can be found 'under the soles of your shoes'. (Suzy and Mark venture under the floors of the houses in Freiberg and New York, and Anna descends into unexplored catacombs beneath the Roman house in *Mother of Tears*).

During the scene in which we are introduced to Mark, we are given a tantalising glimpse of the Third Mother, the most beautiful and cruel of the three, the Mother of Tears. She makes her presence known to Mark as he sits in a lecture brooding over Rose's letter. The actress who portrayed the Mother of Tears in this scene – and also in the scene where she is glimpsed briefly driving past a murder scene in a taxi – was Ania Pieroni. Her appearance and subsequent death in Argento's next film *Tenebrae* would lead to speculation that the director, in killing off her character of the sexy shoplifter, had also killed any notion of returning to complete his trilogy.

Style/Technical

The Neo-Gothic look of *Inferno* and its bewitching and dreamlike atmosphere is the logical progression from that of *Suspiria*. Argento wanted the two films to be very different in tone and feel and, to a great extent, he achieved this. *Inferno*'s lighting scheme is somewhat more subdued than that of *Suspiria*, but the whole film is beautifully lit, bathed in striking blues, reds and ambers. This ethereal lighting by cinematographer Romano Albani, who would go on to lens the somewhat more subdued and darker-looking *Phenomena*, denotes the supernatural and mystically charged atmosphere that possesses the abode of the Mother of Darkness. As the film progresses and her evil begins to spread, this incredible lighting bleeds out into the everyday realities of various characters' lives in the guise of lightning storms, street lamps and police lights.

All the constraints associated with plausibility are cast aside by Argento as he once again seems keen to submerge the viewer in another assault on the senses. If one thought the plot of *Suspiria* was rather loose, that of *Inferno* is even more so. Aside perhaps from the films of David Lynch, it is quite possibly the closest a film has ever come to capturing the very essence of a nightmare on celluloid. Events move along in a stream-of-consciousness-style narrative, and the film unfolds like a dark visual poem.

In charge of production design was Argento regular Giuseppe Bassan. His beautifully intimidating set designs take on a life of their own, and indeed the house's very dimensions seem to change throughout the course of the film. Warped logic holds sway not only over the story but over the sets too. Like Escher's 'Relativity', rooms and hallways exist where, logically speaking, they should not; the submerged ballroom Rose finds under the flooded cellar highlights the supernatural attributes of the house and its evil inhabitant; the fact that it appears to have water for its foundations renders it even more creepy and otherworldly. As in *Suspiria*, the sets in *Inferno* dwarf the actors manoeuvring around them.

Argento's camerawork here continues to build upon its wild reputation. At one stage it assumes the point of view of sound waves, moving towards an air duct in a waving motion as the fiendish inhabitants of the house eavesdrop on Mark and Elise's secret conversation.

Mario Bava, another dark genius and purveyor of Italian shock-cinema, assisted Argento on *Inferno* with the special effects. He and his son Lamberto, who also worked as first assistant director, created miniature sets and skylines but, contrary to popular belief, did not film the underwater ballroom scene – this was filmed in a water tank in Rome by Gianlorenzo Battaglia. Bava designed the effects in the climax where the Mother of Darkness bursts through a mirror to reveal her true form, a giant skeletal death-head.

Themes

As in *Suspiria*, *Inferno* is also awash with distinct Jungian imagery. The film's very title is somewhat misleading in that the images it conjures up might suggest that hellish fires abound within the story. The complete opposite is actually true and, while there is indeed a cathartic, fiery inferno at the climax, the rest of the film bathes itself in images of water and all the connotations that come with them. In dream analysis, water is associated with maternal, nurturing instincts but also with devouring power. This encapsulates the Three Mothers and subverts the notion of the 'nurturing mother' into something more sinister and overbearing. Puddles and rain storms appear throughout the film and various key set pieces are also submerged in water: the eerie flooded ballroom, Kazanian's watery death in Central Park and Mark's bizarre dream of a lapping tide on a distant shore.

Other images throughout *Inferno* are decidedly more Freudian in association, but still highlight the connection with the 'maternal'. The various womb-like tunnels, passageways and corridors that riddle the house; the vaginal gap in the floor where Mark finds a vital clue to the dark secret of the house; and the moment when Rose lowers herself into a mysterious orifice in the cellar: all these create breathtaking images associated with the 'monstrous mother' and realms of the unknown. These images of characters entering water and lowering themselves into darkness recall Mark's search of a flooded basement in *Deep Red* and of various other instances in both *The Church* and *The Sect* when characters return to water – traditionally a source of life, but, in the case of Argento's dark waters, a harbourer of terrible secrets that consume all.

The fairytale motifs present in *Suspiria* are also rife throughout *Inferno*. Rose and Mark, following a scattering of clues, and at one stage a trail of blood spots, are akin to Hansel and Gretel. At various times, like the characters in *Suspiria*, they seem overtly childlike and naïve, with both of them connected to learning and studying through their respective careers. Several shots of a paper-doll chain with the heads being snipped off by scissors also have distinct connotations of childhood. The pair also wander around the vast interior of the house with a wide-eyed innocence. The Countess Elise, a sickly, neurotic character, is reliant on an overbearing and smothering manservant to care for her while her husband is away. The presence of a powerful witch harbouring malicious intent towards the sleuths highlights this connection with fairy stories, as does the opening of the film when Rose reads through the pages of a book about the Three Mothers, a narrator explaining to us that they are more like wicked 'stepmothers, incapable of creating life'. Riddles and puzzles are peppered throughout the story and characters often speak in cryptic terms; at one stage Kazanian states 'I don't like riddles'.

Fairytale simplicity is all that can explain the 'heart medicine' Mark is given by the sinister housekeeper when he collapses after a creepy encounter in the cellar. Art and various other aesthetic objects, such as ornate door handles, statues and mantelpieces, all seem to indicate and predict the doom of various characters who accidentally break them, as demonstrated when Rose smashes her crystal door handle and is shortly afterwards garrotted by a fiendish attacker. Argento appears to be nodding to *Psycho* (1960) with the premature death of Rose, a character we initially assume to be the protagonist.

Again referencing inspirational artists, Argento includes various shots of ants crawling throughout the structure of the house and onto a character's hand at one stage, not only indicating the rancid state of affairs but also referencing Dali and his association of ants with death and decay.

The characters in *Inferno*, like most of Argento's protagonists, are involved in the arts: Rose is a poet; Mark and Sara are music students, also connected with learning and indicating that the search for forbidden knowledge in Argento's films can only lead to death and destruction. This deadly, almost Lovecraftian, desire for knowledge and the severe penalties it carries stalks the characters of *Inferno*. Sara is attacked in a library when she discovers *The Three Mothers* by Varelli. Varelli himself, in breaking what alchemists refer to as 'silentium', is damned by his actions. The moon is essentially another character in *Inferno*; seemingly omniscient, it peers in through countless windows, no doubt controlling the waters that flow throughout the building (and perhaps the menstrual cycles of its female inhabitants, such is its dark power).

As in *Deep Red* and later on in *Opera* and *Trauma*, Argento enjoys inserting shots of various animals, particularly his favourites, lizards, snacking on insects and reminding us of the malevolent predators at large in the story.

Drapes feature again in the scenes where Sara enters the creepy library and when Rose and Elise are pursued through the house by an unseen stalker.

Music

Inferno's soundtrack was composed by Keith Emerson of prog-rock outfit Emerson, Lake and Palmer. Rock fan Argento wanted something that would equal the intensity and grandeur of Goblin's scores when, due to personal problems, that band was unable to score *Inferno*.

Emerson delivers a dazzling score, incorporating piano, synthesisers, operatic vocals and a 90-piece orchestra. Sinister and delicate piano motifs wrap themselves around rich choral excerpts and, as events progress, the music becomes increasingly deranged and bombastic until it resembles an audacious rock opera. Emerson composed the score to rough cuts of the film and Argento gave him free rein. His only insistence was that the musician used Verdi's *Nabucco*, which he does to delirious effect in a 5–4 time arrangement accompanying the scene where Sara takes a taxi to the library. Argento also uses Verdi's 'Chorus of Hebrew Slaves' to creepy effect in the scene where Sara and Carlo are murdered during the power cut in her flat.

The score for *Inferno* was recorded directly to film and Argento was so impressed that he brought Emerson in again to score Soavi's *The Church*. This proved to be a bad experience for Emerson, as he claims he was never given credit for his services, and the two haven't worked together since.

Trivia

The taxi driver (Fulvio Mingozzi) who takes Sara to the library is also the grumpy driver of Suzy's taxi in *Suspiria*. His character seems to be some sort of Charon or ferryman figure, transporting the damned to their dark destinations.

Verdict

Another garish and nightmarish voyage into the realms of terror, *Inferno* is as breathtakingly beautiful and intense as *Suspiria* and unravels with even less logic. The stuff of pure nightmares.

RETURN TO YELLOW

Tenebrae (1982)

'Pervert... filthy slimy pervert.'

Directed/Written by: Dario Argento
Co-written by: George Kemp
Produced by: Claudio Argento
Music by: Claudio Simonetti, Fabio Pignatelli & Massimo Morante
Cinematography: Luciano Tovoli
Edited by: Franco Fraticelli
Art Director: Giuseppe Bassan
Special Effects: Giovanni Corridori
Cast: Anthony Franciosa (Peter Neal), John Saxon (Bulmer), Daria Nicolodi (Anne), Giuliano Gemma (Captain Giermani), John Steiner (Cristiano Berti), Ania Pieroni (Elsa Manni), Mirella D'Angelo (Tilde)
Also known as: *Tenebre, Unsane, Under the Eyes of the Assassin*

Synopsis

Horror writer Peter Neal arrives in Rome to promote his new best-seller. Unfortunately for Peter, though, a deranged fan has taken his latest book as the main inspiration for a series of ghoulish murders. As Peter and the police try to track down the killer before he strikes again, Peter becomes increasingly linked to events and begins to lose his grip on reality.

Background

Audiences assumed that Argento would complete his 'Three Mothers' trilogy after *Inferno*; however, feeling the pressure and the need to once again defy expectations, Argento did the unexpected and made a swift return to the contemporary *giallo* film, shooting *Tenebrae* in May 1982.

After the success of *Suspiria*, Argento spent time in LA. There, he became the target of a crazed fan's obsession and received a number of threatening phone calls from this fanatical stalker who wanted to harm Argento in a way that reflected how much the director's work had affected him. This created the spark of an idea about an artist being punished for their art. Critics have often suggested that the character of Peter Neal serves as an alter-ego for Argento in the film. Indeed, a number of debates between characters about violence and misogyny in film and literature mirror Argento's own opinions on such matters, highlighted in the argument between Peter and Tilde about his latest 'misogynistic' novel.

Comments

A number of similar elements that weave through *Inferno* and *Tenebrae* led audiences to believe that the latter was an unofficial sequel. *Tenebrae* also begins with someone reading from a book – Neal's fictional novel – and the actress who portrayed the Mother of Tears in *Inferno*, Ania Pieroni, is also the sexy shoplifter in *Tenebrae*.

The film was released outside Italy in various cut forms and banned outright in the UK, having been added to the growing list of 'video nasties'.

Christopher Walken is rumoured to have been considered for the part of troubled writer Peter Neal and Theresa Russell dubbed the character of Anne (Daria Nicolodi) in the international version. John Saxon made his return to the *giallo* in *Tenebrae*, 20 years after filming Mario Bava's seminal *The Girl Who Knew Too Much* (1963).

The Rome depicted in *Tenebrae* is not the Rome usually portrayed in films; Argento is careful to avoid shots of landmarks and baroque architecture. Instead it is presented as an anonymous city, devoid of its typical characteristics and full of high rises brimming with a modern sheen, perhaps suggesting that the events unfolding in the story could happen anywhere.

Style/Technical

Argento wanted a cutting edge and cool contemporary look for *Tenebrae*. Setting the story in the near future and not in the present day, the director, wanting a crystal-clear and precise style, turned once again to cinematographer Luciano Tovoli (*Suspiria*) to create the film's cold, stark and semi-futuristic look. 'Tenebrae' is Latin for shadows/darkness, and Argento claims that it is the 'darkness' of the human soul he is exploring throughout the film.

Like *Inferno* and the images that title conjures up, *Tenebrae*'s rather misleading title showcases the director's determination to defy expectations and shun convention.

Strangely, every scene is almost over-lit, with light flooding into each shot from a particular onscreen source, as though Argento were telling us that there is nowhere to hide from the darkness of the soul except in the darkest place of all: one's own mind. Tovoli claims that *Tenebrae* was perhaps even tougher to light than *Suspiria* and the vaguely futuristic look was a challenge he relished tackling. The result is a striking looking film bathed in bright whites, with sporadic slashes of bright primary colours.

The prowling camerawork in *Tenebrae* is nothing short of astounding, with one sequence in particular standing out in Argento's body of work as showcasing his passion for technical prowess and breathtaking visuals. Utilising a Louma crane specially imported from Paris (and marking the first time such equipment was used in an Italian production), Argento's camera scales a victim's house in one seamless take, navigating walls, roofs and peering in through windows, in a set piece that effortlessly exposes the penetrability of a seemingly secure home. Initially it appears that what we are seeing is presented as the intruder's point of view; however, when the intruder actually moves into the shot from below a window on the ground floor, we realise that it was just a case of Argento playing with perception. The aerial gymnastics performed by the camera would appear to exist purely for their own sake and do not represent the movements of the killer. This suggests that Argento is perhaps alluding once again to the voyeuristic tendencies of the audience.

Argento again situates the camera in the place of the killer and we are forced to watch the bloody murders from this viewpoint.

Themes

Tenebrae is a highly reflexive film and Argento actively examines and reflects on themes that reappear throughout his oeuvre with a savage precision. Freudian psychological transfer, sexual deviancy, repressed trauma, brutal and stylised violence and the allegedly sinister effects of art on society: all are on display in this twisted story.

Tenebrae is also slightly unusual because there are actually two killers operating separately and with very different motives: Peter Neal, a typical Argento protagonist – an American writer visiting Italy – kills to conceal repressed memories of a murder he committed years ago, due to psychosexual anguish; Cristiano Berti, however, is inspired to kill by literature, in an attempt to cleanse society of those he considers to be morally depraved.

Usually in Argento's films, characters meet horrifying deaths at the hands of sadistic killers because they have discovered, knowingly or not, a clue to the killer's identity and motive. What's slightly different about *Tenebrae* is that Argento intended all of the violence to seem random, completely unmitigated and representative of modern fears. Of course, *Tenebrae* does feature a killer with serious psychological issues due to a repressed traumatic event – sexual humiliation in this case – that has come back to haunt him, a permanent staple in all of Argento's *giallo* movies. Interestingly, *Tenebrae* is also regarded as one of Argento's most controversial films, mainly due to the fact that the violent content is stylised in such a way as to render it almost sexual. The eroticisation of violence is distinctly apparent, with an almost iconic slew of beautiful female victims sporting detached performances and an almost sexual response to having sharp implements thrust into their vulnerable flesh. The killer's Freudian flashbacks enhance the sexual nature of the murders and, in almost 'slasher movie' terms, many of the victims are beautiful, sexually active women, seemingly being punished for their promiscuity. Indeed, it is their sexuality that prompts the first killer, Cristiano Berti, to dispatch them. The severely conservative TV critic is revealed to be the murderer of the film's first female victims. He killed them because of their 'perversions', i.e. their sexual activity. His character is hypocrisy personified. Peter Neal, after writing about crimes, begins to re-enact them – killing Berti and anyone else who comes close to discovering his identity.

While accusations of misogyny have been hurled at Argento throughout his career, particularly in relation to *Tenebrae*, these claims become somewhat distorted when one takes into account that the sexually alluring woman featured in the Freudian flashbacks is actually portrayed by a transsexual, actress Eva Robins. This subversive manipulation on Argento's part echoes the character of Carlos's transvestite lover in *Deep Red* (portrayed by a woman) and underlines Argento's interest in gender and the blurred line that often defines it.

Through the dialogue in *Tenebrae*, Argento addresses these accusations directly and reveals his opinions about violence in films. When questioned by the police after pages of his book are found stuffed into the mouth of one of the victims, Neal retorts, 'If someone is killed with a Smith & Wesson revolver, do you interview the president of Smith & Wesson?' This is Argento's response to those who accuse his films, and horror films in general, of having an impact on the violence so prevalent in our society.

The fact that Berti was inspired to kill by Neal's latest novel is also important. With this concept, Argento explores the relationship between art and life, and how the two reflect each other. The murderous actions in the film repeat passages that are contained within the novel. Berti's murders are a sort of homage to Neal's work and Neal's murders are his fictionalisation of reality; he even utters, 'It was like a book. A book!' Highlighting, in a somewhat humorous way, the 'harmfulness' of art, Peter is impaled with a spiky sculpture by Anne at the end of the film when she rushes into the house, accidentally knocking it over. This recalls Sam's entrapment under a huge sculpture in *The Bird with the Crystal Plumage*, Suzy's crystal weapon at the end of *Suspiria* and the paintings that trigger psychosis in *The Bird with the Crystal Plumage* and *The Stendhal Syndrome*.

Argento addresses the notion that we all have the potential to give in to the darkness within our souls in an astonishing shot towards the end of the film. After Inspector Germani returns to the house, still thinking that Peter is dead, he is filmed standing in the room in a medium shot. He notices something on the floor and bends down to retrieve it; as he sinks out of the shot, Peter Neal is revealed to be standing directly behind him and the image almost resembles someone shedding a skin. Argento is perhaps suggesting with this shot that there is a killer lurking within everyone and we all have the capacity to do vile and corrupt things, as well as highlighting the recurring theme of psychological transference within his films.

Tenebrae serves as a reflexive commentary on Argento's work and the reception it usually receives, and indeed its influences, especially detective fiction and how Argento subverts the usual methods of rational deduction. The *giallo* film itself has its roots firmly in literature, albeit that of a fairly pulpy tradition. Amongst the works and authors referenced in *Tenebrae* are Agatha Christie, Mickey Spillane,

Rex Stout and Ed McBain. Argento also nods to *Black Angel* (1946), directed by Roy William Neill and adapted from a novel by Cornell Woolrich, in which a man who sets out to clear the name of a murder suspect learns that he himself is the perpetrator of the crime.

The reflexivity also stretches to Peter Neal's first 'death' scene in which he fakes his own suicide with a blunt razor and fake blood. Argento would appear to be prodding the audience and saying that, as sickening as his murder scenes are, ultimately they are just special effects. This pondering of the art of illusion and actually revealing how the effects work is a sly strategy Argento employs, lifting us temporarily out of the reality of the film and allowing us to consider why we enjoy watching such gory events on film. It's no coincidence that many of the victims gaze into the camera directly at us, not only implying our involvement in the violence but also reminding us that it is happening for our entertainment, as Argento deals head on with the critical reception of his films.

This 'gaze' also serves to highlight Argento's preoccupation with voyeurism and spectacle. As in the later *Giallo*, the killer photographs the aftermath of his attacks, with beautiful corpses staring blankly into his lens. The camera also occupies his line of sight on many occasions, stalking and mutilating victims. The passive gaze of many onlookers is also on fierce display, as evident in the scenes featuring Bullmer's murder in a bustling city square, the vagrant witnessing the murder of the shoplifter and Gianni witnessing Berti's bloody execution. Argento makes it clear we need to be aware of our own passivity as an audience.

The fetishisation of weapons and murderous implements occurs frequently in *Tenebrae*, particularly in the flashback sequences featuring a woman 'orally raping' a man with the heel of her bright-red stilettos. The insanity of the killer in *Tenebrae* is blatantly the result of sexual deviation, and a number of critics have pointed out that the overall sensuality inherent in *Tenebrae*'s imagery and story sets it apart from Argento's previous *gialli*.

Music

The music in *Tenebrae* is characteristic of many Italian horror movies in the 1980s and represents a typical Euro-horror soundtrack, based around prog-rock compositions and heavily reliant on synthesisers and electronics. While Goblin were once again responsible for scoring the music to accompany Argento's stylish images of death and violence, the band members are all credited for their contributions separately. By this stage, the personal problems they were experiencing had come to a head and the band had essentially split.

Argento plays with our perceptions in *Tenebrae* through audio trickery too. In one scene, Tilde yells at her girlfriend to turn off the music, which we had assumed was merely the soundtrack of the film. When we cut to her girlfriend upstairs, she crosses the room and lifts the needle from the record player. The music, both diegetic and non-diegetic, stops instantly and we realise it wasn't just there for atmosphere, but because one of the characters was also listening to it.

Verdict

Tenebrae has a serpentine narrative that becomes even more complex and convoluted as the story unfolds, yet it manages to draw you in and become utterly compelling as Argento plays with notions of perception and perspective and explores the potentially fatal influence of art on its audience. All with typically atmospheric and stylish aplomb and containing some of the maestro's most iconic imagery.

Phenomena (1985)

Directed/Written/Produced by: Dario Argento
Co-written by: Franco Ferrini
Music by: Simon Boswell & Goblin
Cinematography: Romano Albani
Edited by: Franco Fraticelli

Production Designers: Maurizio Garrone, Nello Giorgetti, Luciano Spa-
doni & Umberto Turco
Special Effects: Luigi Cozzi & Sergio Stivaletti
Cast: Jennifer Connelly (Jennifer Corvino), Donald Pleasence (Professor
John McGregor), Daria Nicolodi (Frau Brückner), Patrick Bauchau (Inspec-
tor Rudolf Geiger), Federica Mastroianni (Sophie), Dalila Di Lazzaro (Head
Mistress), Fiore Argento (Vera Brandt)
Also known as: *Creepers*

Synopsis

American schoolgirl Jennifer Corvino is sent to an exclusive boarding
school in Switzerland while her actor father works on a new movie.
Jennifer finds it difficult to settle in because of her sleepwalking
and latent telepathy with insects. She finds out that a serial killer
has been stalking the area and killing young girls for some time.
Befriending an ageing entomologist, Jennifer becomes caught up in
the grim proceedings and must hone her secret abilities to stop the
killer before she becomes the next victim.

Background

Phenomena was the first film produced by Argento's film company
DAC – Dario Argento Company (later changed to ADC). Just before
the film went into production, Argento's father, Salvatore, who had
worked with his son since his first film, retired from his career as an
executive producer due to poor health. Argento's brother Claudio did
not return to work with him on *Phenomena* either, due to conflicts
between the brothers after *Tenebrae*.

This film also marked the first time that Argento would work
with his regular writing partner Franco Ferrini, as well as the acting
debut of the director's daughter, Fiore, and Michele Soavi's debut as
Argento's assistant director.

The story was inspired by an article in an American newspaper
about the alleged affinity insects share with mediums, sleepwalk-

ers and schizophrenics, a concept Argento flirted with in *Deep Red*. Shooting began in August 1984 with a budget of $4 million, and also marked the first time Argento directed a film entirely in English.

Comments

Phenomena is often, rather unfairly, regarded by many as the absolute nadir of Argento's career. It is in fact an encyclopaedic compilation of elements from his previous work, most notably *Suspiria* and *Deep Red*. *Phenomena* can be viewed as a stepping stone in Argento's canon of work – with this film he tried to amalgamate his *giallo* films with the supernatural tinges of his 'Three Mothers' trilogy. The resulting meshing of typical *giallo* traits with overt paranormal trimmings is interesting, if not always successful. *Phenomena* is also one of Argento's cruellest and most nightmarish movies, especially towards the end when logic is dispelled completely and all we are left with is a series of sadistic set pieces that segue from one to the next in a way that gives itself up completely to the irrationality of nightmares.

Argento at one stage believed, rather contrarily, that *Phenomena* epitomised his work more than any of his other films. While it is not without its rather iconic moments, such as Jennifer bursting to the surface of a pool of decomposing bodies and the pop-promo introductions to her sleepwalking scenes, it is certainly not one of Argento's strongest films.

Jennifer Connelly was 14 at the time of filming and had just finished work on Leone's *Once Upon a Time in America*. In *Phenomena* she portrays a 13-year-old girl. Argento had also wanted to feature pre-adolescent characters in Suspiria, but it was deemed too controversial given the subject matter of that film.

Peter Ustinov was tipped to play the role of entomologist John McGregor before it went to Donald Pleasence, and Isabella Rossellini was offered the role of the stern headmistress but, due to scheduling conflicts, turned it down.

Released in the States in severely cut form as *Creepers*, a number of pivotal scenes were removed, including the medical tests on Jennifer, the voiceover that introduces her to the audience, and the scene detailing her psychic empathy with the larvae that reveal to her where Sophie's mutilated body lies. This rendered it a confusing, nonsensical mess – though many have argued that *Phenomena* was a confusing, nonsensical mess to begin with!

Style/Technical

Phenomena has a dark and ominous look, due to it being one of the first films to use fibre optics as a light source. The film is bathed in deep blues, blacks and whites. Argento shuns the hyper-reality evident in the likes of *Tenebrae* and *The Bird with the Crystal Plumage* and the Gothic majesty of *Suspiria* and *Deep Red*. Many scenes are set at night and Argento really makes the most of his locations; the way he films the serene and oddly sinister Swiss landscapes and picturesque houses dotted throughout belies a certain dread. The 'Swiss Transylvania' he strives to convey is fully realised. The various shots of quaint and secluded cottages evoke tales of lost children and gingerbread houses of classic fairytales.

The sound design of the film highlights the sinister wind that constantly blows in this part of Switzerland. Dubbed the 'föhn' by locals, it is said that this 'rain shadow' wind allegedly drives people insane. With its constant howling and its seemingly omniscient presence throughout *Phenomena*, it enhances the deliciously dark and foreboding atmosphere. It also echoes the mysterious spectral winds that blew through Mater Tenebrarum's house in *Inferno*.

Argento indulges in many strange point-of-view shots in the film. We not only see events from the deranged killer's perspective, as the camera races after victims, we are also aligned with the victims' point of view as they glance back at their sadistic pursuer. Argento also films from the POV of an array of insects, notably in the shot where the larvae on Sophie's glove show Jennifer where Sophie's body is and the screen is split up into a kaleidoscope of viewpoints. These bizarre shots serve to highlight Argento's preoccupation with how we view the world around us and the act of 'looking'.

The insect footage took several months to film and, aside from the scenes in which Jennifer follows a luridly glowing firefly, those featuring the Great Sarcophagus Fly and the exterior shot of the school as an enormous swarm of flies descends upon it, no special effects or stop-motion effects were applied to the film. The exterior shot of the school besieged by flies was created by filming ground coffee swirling in water and layering it on top of the shot of the school.

Echoing the underwater ballroom of *Inferno*, *Phenomena* also features an eerie underwater sequence where Jennifer, flinging herself into the lake from her burning boat, encounters the not-quite-dead body of Frau Brückner's monstrous child, the scene lit from above by the fire spreading along the surface of the water.

The camerawork in *Phenomena*, while slightly more restrained than that of previous Argento films, is still quite breathtaking. The film opens with an impressive crane shot that rises above dark trees to peer at the isolated Alpine landscape of dense forests and white-peaked purple mountains beyond, setting the mood perfectly for the cold and sadistic opening murder that follows.

Astounding dream imagery is laced throughout the film, most notably in the logic-defying sleepwalking set pieces where Jennifer traverses buildings and wanders through forests guided by fireflies, dressed in an almost ethereal white sleeping gown.

As mentioned, towards the end of the film when the narrative becomes less logical and more dreamlike, Argento really lets his imagination loose, and the images we see are bizarre and disturbing; notably in the scenes when Jennifer is frantically trying to escape from Brückner by crawling into a hole in the floor (recalling Mark and Rose in *Inferno*), pulling a telephone with her. As she crawls along the tunnels beneath the house, she descends deeper and deeper into a nightmarish landscape, tumbling from one dark space into another as she attempts to use the phone, which at one stage begins to ring ominously.

The demise of Frau Brückner is surely one of the most savage and cruel Argento has ever dreamed up, the absurdity of it only adding to the sadism. As she makes one last attempt to kill Jennifer, Brückner is leapt on by Inga, McGregor's chimpanzee, who proceeds to slash her to death with a cut-throat razor.

Daria Nicolodi has stated that she had a dreadful experience making this film with Argento. Their relationship was disintegrating rapidly and the events that befall her character in *Phenomena* lend credence to suggestions that the downfall of the pairs' romance can be traced throughout their work together. Apparently her death scene as it appears in the film did not appear in the original script, suggesting perhaps that Argento sadistically dreamt it up to gain some form of catharsis.

Themes

Reoccurring themes and preoccupations that litter Argento's previous work are scattered throughout *Phenomena*, with seemingly wild abandon.

It shares a few similarities with *Suspiria*, notably its young female protagonist staying in a boarding school in a foreign land and the fairy-tale-like narration that introduces her, which oddly doesn't appear until about 15 minutes into the film. Her classmates don't like her because she is an outsider and they are petty and vindictive towards her.

She displays psychic tendencies, like those possessed by Helga in *Deep Red*, and she can communicate with insects. The psychic ability of insects is also a topic of discussion in *Deep Red*.

Insects are a particular interest of Argento's and they are present in a number of his films: the maggots in *Suspiria*, the ants in *Inferno*, and the psychic links they share with mediums are discussed in *Deep Red*. They also form part of the title of *Four Flies on Grey Velvet*.

Jennifer is another of Argento's strong female protagonists, struggling to survive amidst strange occurrences and alienation. She initially views her special abilities as a curse and something that marks her as abnormal. When she finally comes to terms with her fate and embraces it, Jennifer is shown emerging from a lake: reborn. It would appear that the ugly duckling she feared she was has bloomed into a beautiful swan. The imagery of rebirth is also evoked during the scene in which Jennifer is examined by the school doctor and he says that her sleepwalking could be signs of a new personality inside her 'trying to emerge', as a butterfly would from a chrysalis.

The sexual anxiety that bleeds into the narrative of *Tenebrae* and which is also laced into the imagery of *Suspiria*, where scantily clad students wander about the school, reappears to a lesser extent here, in the form of the adolescent Jennifer. Her blossoming sexuality arouses not only the killer's interests, but that of the insects she communicates with; in one scene they bombard her with mating calls and displays of virility.

Jennifer is called 'Beelzebub' ('Lord of the Flies') by her headmistress, who thinks she is mentally ill and encourages the other girls to ostracise her.

The absurd image of Jennifer using a fly in a box to guide her to the killer's lair is strangely engrossing, and if the audience gives itself up to the illogicality that eventually strangles proceedings in *Phenomena*, they will be treated to some of the strangest imagery and concepts Argento has ever concocted.

During her bouts of sleepwalking, Jennifer witnesses the sadistic killing of a young girl and the brief glimpse of the killer's face haunts her throughout the rest of the film as she struggles to make sense of what she saw, all the while trying to convince people she did not imagine it. This is another example of an Argento protagonist struggling to recall a significant clue to identify a killer.

The 'monstrous mother' returns here in the form of Frau Brückner, with her deformed and psychotic offspring. Her child is described as having abnormal genetic make-up because of the ghastly way in which he was conceived – Brückner worked as a nurse in a psychiatric hospital and was raped by the criminally insane inmates. This abnormality at genetic level recalls the killer's criminally inclined chromosomes in *Cat O'Nine Tails*. In a perverse subversion of Carlo and Martha in *Deep Red*, Brückner has to kill to keep the murders of her son a secret.

Further issues with maternal figures are raised when Jennifer tells Sophie about her mother leaving, and how her father and she now depend only on each other. This sad story apparently reflects Argento's own experiences with his mother when growing up as a boy.

When Brückner's son's terrible face is eventually revealed as Jennifer glimpses his reflection in a mirror, the moment calls to mind the sinister elements of mirrors explored in *Deep Red*, when a mirror contains and distorts the identity of Martha, and also *Inferno*, when Mater Tenebrarum bursts through a mirror to reveal her true form. The mirrors that adorn many of the walls in Brückner's house are covered with drapes and sheets, a warning that to look into them or to see what horrors they reflect is to enter forbidden territory.

Jennifer assumes the role of detective in *Phenomena*; the police, as is quite usual in Argento's films, don't really seem to do very much, except when Inspector Geiger shows up towards the end to conveniently rescue Jennifer from a pool of decaying bodies in the basement of Frau Brückner's creepy house. Until his death, Jennifer is encouraged by John McGregor to explore her telepathic abilities, and the pair forms an unlikely duo, recalling the tranquil and touching relationships at the heart of *Cat O'Nine Tails*, *Deep Red* and much later in *The Card Player*.

Allusions to literature also crop up in *Phenomena*, particularly in the scene where Geiger visits the psychiatric hospital and, as he descends in the elevator, is told that the farther down they go, the crazier the inmates, evoking Dante's descent into the various levels of hell.

Music

Phenomena's soundtrack consists of several atmospheric pieces by Bill Wyman (The Rolling Stones) and former Goblin members Claudio Simonetti and Fabio Pignatelli, combining synthesiser-rock and operatic vocals. Tracks from Iron Maiden and Motorhead, amongst others, are used inappropriately and decimate the mood. Argento's love for rock metal would also find its way into the score for *Opera*, where it sounds just as ear-splitting.

Trivia

The costumes in *Phenomena* were designed by Armani.

Verdict

Despite various astounding segments, *Phenomena* as a whole often falls short, at times its story as ludicrous as Pleasence's Scottish accent. It appears to be a scattershot of Argento's preoccupations and recurring themes thrown together to form a full-blown fantasy movie with lashings of shocking violence and spirituality. An interesting if slightly flawed entry in Argento's oeuvre.

Opera (1987)

Directed/Written/Produced by: Dario Argento
Co-written by: Franco Ferrini
Music by: Claudio Simonetti
Cinematography: Ronnie Taylor BSC
Edited by: Franco Fraticelli
Production Designer: Davide Bassan
Special Effects: Sergio Stivaletti
Cast: Cristina Marsillach (Betty), Ian Charleson (Marco), Urbano Barberini (Inspector Alan Santini), Daria Nicolodi (Myra), Coralina Cataldi-Tassoni (Julia), William McNamara (Stefan)
Also known as: *Terror at the Opera*

Synopsis

When opera diva Myra Chekova storms out of rehearsals and is knocked down by a car, her understudy Betty takes her place and becomes the target of an obsessed fan who seems to have strange links to her childhood. He begins killing those close to Betty, forcing her to watch in the most sadistic way imaginable, in a warped attempt to make her love him.

Background

Opera began shooting in May 1987 and was the most expensive of Argento's films, with a budget of $8 million. Once again the director was assisted in writing the screenplay by Franco Ferrini and the cast and crew featured many Argento regulars, including Daria Nicolodi, Sergio Stivaletti and Claudio Simonetti. This also marked the first time Argento worked with the notable cinematographer Ronnie Taylor.

Opera is notorious for being Argento's toughest production; behind the scenes the director's personal life was in turmoil. His tempestuous relationship with Nicolodi had finally come to a bitter end. His father, who had been ill for quite some time, sadly passed away during filming. The darkness in Argento's personal life seems to have bled into every frame of *Opera*, which stands as one of his bleakest works.

The death of actor Ian Charleson shortly after the film was completed (Charleson had also been in a car crash prior to filming) was also a blow to Argento, and superstitious rumours about the use of *Macbeth* as the opera in the film haunted the director.

Comments

Argento has wryly stated that *Opera* is his response to films such as Martin Scorsese's *After Hours* (1985), which, ironically, Scorsese had actually filmed in homage to Argento's work. In any case, the story is a loose adaptation of one of the director's favourite films, *The Phantom of the Opera* (1925), which he would later remake to disastrous effect.

Argento had been approached by the Sferisterio Theatre in Macerata to direct a production of Verdi's opera *Rigoletto* and, with the assistance of special-effects man Sergio Stivaletti, the director set about planning how he would do it.

Amongst his ideas was the decision to change the character of the Duke into a vampiric pervert. However, once purists realised his intentions, they simply would not allow the production to go ahead. The backstabbing and bickering Argento encountered behind the scenes of this short-lived project went some way to inspire the story of *Opera*, the first draft of which had to be heavily edited due to its length and insanely violent set pieces.

Argento's volatile relationship with previous actors would be relived throughout *Opera* in his troubled rapport with leading lady Cristina Marsillach.

Marsillach was allegedly very demanding and contrary in her dealings with Argento, something he resented her for. *Legend*'s (1985) Mia Sara was at one stage considered for the part. A more positive experience for the director, however, came in the form of his relationship with Ian Charleson, who, unknown to Argento at the time, based his performance on the maestro at work.

When the film premiered at Cannes, it wasn't well received due to the atrocious dubbing – especially that of Detective Santini (Urbano Barbarini), whose rather effeminate and inappropriate dub suits neither the actor nor the character. His voice was re-looped and, as a result, much of his dialogue sounds echoic and quite odd.

Style/Technical

Argento employed state-of-the-art equipment to realise his aria of violence. The camerawork in *Opera* is amongst Argento's most graceful and fluid. Whether it's depicting the killer's point of view as he stalks his victims backstage, or that of the ravens circling the auditorium, descending gradually to seek out the killer seated in the audience, the camerawork is breathtaking and dazzling. Argento and Taylor hung the camera from a rig in the ceiling for these impressive birds'-eye views of the opera house in the scene were the killer is revealed. The dizzying shots have to be seen to be believed.

Argento had accepted an offer to direct the first Fiat Cromo commercial in order to experiment with the latest film equipment. Ronnie Taylor also worked on this advert and the two bonded through their mutual respect for each other's work, though Taylor would later admit to feeling very squeamish when filming the bloody murders Argento dreamt up.

Taylor's crisp photography and Antonio Scaramuzza's flawless Steadicam work add to the chilly atmosphere and, although they often bring us into the centre of the action, there is something quite detached and clinical about the film, largely due to the highly realistic style Argento insisted it be shot in. As realistic and modern as *Opera* is, however, it is still steeped in an elegant look and drenched in the foreboding and lavish atmosphere one would expect in an Argento film.

Glimpses of fairytale-like turrets in the flashbacks hark back to the baroque architecture of *Suspiria* and *Inferno*, though Argento expresses restraint in most of the other sets in *Opera*, aside from the flamboyant set design of the onscreen opera *Macbeth*.

Argento really pushed boundaries in terms of onscreen violence in *Opera*. The film features some of his most grisly and shocking deaths, including the stabbing of Betty's sweet boyfriend Stefan. Argento films this murder in unrelenting detail. In one shot we see the killer's knife thrust so far into Stefan's throat we can see the blade gleaming inside his mouth.

Curious angles and viewpoints drip into almost every scene, including a shot filmed from inside a plughole as Betty pours vile perfume, sent to her by Myra Chekova, down the sink. In the film's opening scene we view the rehearsals of *Macbeth* from the point of view of its diva, Myra Chekova, as she storms out onto the street.

At various stages the camera vibrates, performs gravity-defying movements, is blindfolded, has eye drops applied and, as mentioned above, is doused in perfume. There are shots of the killer's brain pulsating in eye-watering detail as the camera throbs in time to an escalating heartbeat. These shots usually signal the presence of the killer before an attack. The camera is never still in *Opera* as it silently prowls around the set, highlighting various sharp implements that could do damage to tender human flesh.

The scene in which Julia is mending Betty's dress features several shots of a razor cutting into material, and at one stage the camera actually sweeps away from Julia, over the scissor-strewn tabletops of the vast dressing room, to peer at her from the other side of the room.

Argento also employs the use of flashbacks and marks them with the almost poetic movements of his gliding camera through dark hallways and up winding stairs.

The colour palette of *Opera* is relentlessly dark and sombre, with only a few flashes of primary-colour madness in the blood-red drapes backstage and in the luridly gleaming neon lights of Betty's hi-fi.

Themes

Perhaps one of Argento's most enduring themes is that of voyeurism and spectatorship. This reaches a coldly logical conclusion in *Opera*, in the sadistic and forced voyeurism of Betty. Tied up and with rows of needles taped under her eyes so she can't close them, she is forced to watch as the killer gruesomely dispatches her friends and colleagues. Betty, of course, like other Argento protagonists such as Marc Daly, Roberto Tobias and Suzy Banyon, is involved in the world of art and is an opera singer.

Argento had grown tired of people covering their eyes and not watching his scenes of opulent violence – violence is one of his defining characteristics as a filmmaker! He doesn't want his audience to shield their vision from the onslaught of shocking images; he wants viewers to submerge themselves in it and join him on his nightmarish odyssey into the darkest shadows of human depravity.

Eye violation is something of a mainstay in Italian horror, with characters in films having the most vulnerable part of their bodies subjected to all manner of gouging, poking and stabbing. Surely the most perfect metaphor for Argento's forced spectatorship, the image of Betty's eyes wide with fear and needles taped under them, is also one of the maestro's most iconic images. This forced spectatorship recalls the, albeit less sadistic, scene in *The Bird with the Crystal Plumage* when Sam is trapped between the glass doors and is forced to watch the attack on Monica.

This fascination with 'looking' and 'seeing', and imagery conjuring up ideas of voyeurism, prevails throughout *Opera*.

The opening shot of the film is the inside of the opera house reflected in the eye of a raven. This obsession with the eye is also evident in the abundant close-up shots of eyes and the killer's use of opera glasses as he watches events from a private box in the opera house, recalling the creepy, mask-wearing Nina in *Four Flies on Grey Velvet*. Eventually the killer's eye is plucked out by an avenging raven and is later seen being devoured by the bird.

Further highlighting this theme is the scene in which Myra peers through a peephole to catch a glimpse of the killer, only for him to shoot through it and right into her eye, flinging her backwards in devastating slow motion. The slow-motion effect recalls the scene in *Four Flies on Grey Velvet* when Nina shoots Roberto and the camera follows the bullet through the air in slow motion, and the similar effect utilised much later in *The Stendhal Syndrome* when Alfredo shoots a woman in the face and we follow the bullet's passage.

Opera features many of the typical *giallo* traits: the killer clad in black leather gloves, repressed trauma, psycho-sexual deviancy and lashings of stylish gore. As in *Tenebrae*, *Opera* also has a distinct air of sexual anxiety about it. The fetishisation of certain imagery, including the leather gloves worn by the killer and the bound and gagged Betty, evokes sadomasochistic bondage games. The motivation for the murders also drips with heavy sexual undertones, and Betty's frigidity stems from seeing her mother bloodthirstily gloating over the savage deaths of innocent women in the dangerous foreplay she practised with the killer.

Reference is made to the alleged promiscuity and nymphomania of opera singers and film directors. Betty's role in the opera is Lady Macbeth, a part that will always be associated with predatory sexuality and blood lust. The costume worn by Betty as Lady Macbeth is kitted out with various studs and chains and, wearing it, she resembles some sort of avant-garde dominatrix.

Flashbacks masquerading as dreams reoccur throughout *Opera*. Betty is haunted by dreams of a man in a black hood torturing and murdering young women. It transpires that these are flashbacks to when Betty, as a young girl, witnessed the killer in action. He murdered to quench Betty's mother's perverse sexual appetite, as she was aroused by these scenes of violence conducted for her appeasement, and revelled in watching others suffer. The killer was essentially a slave to her, a submissive partner in a warped relationship that played out like a sadomasochistic Gothic nightmare.

These half-remembered, repressed memories that Betty mistakes for dreams are similar to those suffered by Carlo in *Deep Red*, Nina in *Four Flies on Grey Velvet*, Monica in *The Bird with the Crystal Plumage*, Peter Neal in *Tenebrae* and Anna in *The Stendhal Syndrome* – all experience flashbacks that interrupt the narrative of the film to allow the audience tantalising glimpses of what experiences they have tried to forget. All of their traumas seem to have sexual connotations too. The flashbacks feature the sound of running water, as though Argento were deliberately linking them with Freud's connection of water to the womb and the maternal. The air duct Betty and Alma seek refuge in recalls the air ducts and crawl spaces in

Inferno, *Phenomena* and *The Church* and the Freudian connotations they had. Drapes also feature heavily in the flashbacks and, as we pass through them into this dark and seedy nightmare, there is no going back.

It's also interesting to note that the time in which *Opera* opened in cinemas was the late 1980s, a time when AIDS cast its dark shadow over the media and public consciousness. The sexuality in *Opera* is cold and sterile, and the film has an almost nihilistic and loveless tone. Even the killer seems to be overly wary, and dons latex gloves over his black leather ones.

Critics have noted similarities between the character of director Marco and Argento. Both are directors of horror films and both have been lambasted by critics for showcasing scenes of sexual perversity and abstract violence. When questioned by Detective Santini about his responsibility, as a purveyor of horror films, in relation to the spate of murders, Marco replies, 'I think it's unwise to use movies as a guide to reality.' This reflexive statement harks back to Argento's opinions on similar matters in *Tenebrae*.

Marco also reads a review of his version of *Macbeth* in which the critic advises him to 'go back to directing horror movies', much like Argento was instructed to do by those who opposed his proposed version of *Rigoletto*.

Interestingly, the actress portraying Marco's lover Marion, Antonella Vitale, was also Argento's partner at the time, further highlighting how Argento blurs the line between reality and art.

Unusually for an Argento film, there is no bloody and cathartic death in store for the villain. He is simply apprehended by the police and dragged off. While it's not hard to guess his identity, our attention is still commanded by the director through his operatic grandeur and flourishes of visual genius.

The lizard featured at the end provides another example of Argento's often cryptic inclusion of shots of these strange animals throughout his work, as evident in *Inferno* and *Trauma* particularly.

The infamous climax of the film has been criticised by Argento's fans for being too fanciful and whimsical. Harking back to Jennifer Corvino in *Phenomena*, Betty is seen cavorting in the Swiss Alps, embracing nature and vowing a life of solitude. Her sanity is now ambiguous and there is no cathartic release for her; she simply seems to psychologically implode. As beautifully filmed as this short segment is, it is mildly ridiculous.

Music

As well as the inclusion of a couple of harsh rock tracks from thrash metal-heads Steel Grave, the soundtrack of *Opera* consists of more subtle and eerie compositions from Simonetti, with another creepy, music-box lullaby. Brian Eno also provides sinister and tranquil incidental music. It goes without saying that *Opera* features a soundtrack fully utilising compositions by the likes of Verdi, Puccini and Bellini to breathtaking effect.

Verdict

Hailed as the director's last masterpiece before a spiral into lesser works, *Opera* is an astounding tour-de-force of majestic visuals and levels of intense violence rarely seen in cinema. If the graceful camerawork doesn't take your breath away, then the scenes of sadistic bloodshed certainly will. Provocative and nightmarishly unforgettable.

DARK DIASPORA

Due occhi diabolici/Two Evil Eyes (1990)
Argento's segment – Il gatto nero/The Black Cat

'Perversity is one of the prime impulses of the heart.'

'It seems whenever you and I meet there's always a body around.'

Directed/Written/Produced by: Dario Argento
Co-written by: Franco Ferrini
Produced by: Claudio Argento
Music by: Pino Donaggio
Cinematography: Beppe Maccari
Edited by: Pasquale Buba
Production Designer: Cletus Anderson
Special Effects: Tom Savini
Cast: Harvey Keitel (Rod Usher), Madeleine Potter (Annabel), John Amos (Detective Inspector LeGrand), Sally Kirkland (Eleonora), Kim Hunter (Gloria Pym), Holter Ford Graham (Christian), Martin Balsam (Mr Pym)

Synopsis

Crime photographer Rod Usher begins a descent into alcoholism and madness when he kills a stray cat his girlfriend takes in. This murder leads to another and Rod struggles to keep a grip on reality, while the seemingly demonic cat harasses him from beyond the grave.

Background

Argento had become increasingly disappointed with the limited distribution his films had been receiving internationally. While his films had always been successful in Italy, Argento hadn't secured a worldwide hit since *Suspiria*. Determined to widen his audience and his reputation, he decided to align himself with other luminaries within the horror genre. *Two Evil Eyes* was initially conceived as a four-part anthology and amongst those approached to participate in the project were John Carpenter, Clive Barker, Stephen King and Wes Craven; however, scheduling conflicts would ensure that these directors were unable to take part in the proposed project. It is notable, however, that several years later John Carpenter and Tobe Hooper would hook up to make the similar portmanteaux-style film *Body Bags* (1993).

Of all the directors Argento contacted, only Romero joined him, marking the second collaboration between the two, the first being Romero's seminal classic *Dawn of the Dead* (1978). Romero received a memorable phone call from Argento, in which the latter announced himself with, 'Hello, George! I am Dario.' Romero initially assumed he would be working alongside Argento in Rome and was surprised to learn that Argento wanted to come to America to make the film. Both directors had just finished films that suffered problematic shoots: *Opera* and *Monkey Shines* (1988) respectively.

The film is based and shot in Pittsburgh and cost $9 million. It was to be a series of firsts for Argento: his first film to be shot with sound, his first to be made outside of Europe, and the first since *Tenebrae* to be produced by his brother Claudio. After the death of their father, the two siblings reconciled and Claudio has produced the majority of Argento's output since.

The cast and crew had to communicate with Argento through interpreter and dialogue coach Ken Gargaro, as his grasp of the English language was still quite weak at this stage. Though he had shot

Phenomena and *Opera* in English, Argento had never worked with an exclusively English-speaking cast and crew before; his previous work was usually filmed without sound and dubbed in post-production with a view to releasing it internationally.

Initially entitled *Edgar Allan Poe*, then *Poe: Metropolitan Horrors*, to give it an edgier, more contemporary sound, the filmmakers eventually decided on the more ambiguous *Two Evil Eyes*.

The cast includes some of the biggest names Argento has ever worked with, most notably Harvey Keitel and Merchant Ivory regular Madeleine Potter. Potter was attracted to the project because of its literary roots and the director apparently admired her for her 'timeless beauty'.

Argento also has a bit of fun with the supporting cast, with the inclusion of several stalwarts of the genre, such as Kim Hunter (*The Seventh Victim* [1943]) and Martin Balsam (*Psycho* [1960]). Many of the actors working on *Two Evil Eyes* were from the stage and all utilised Stanislavsky's methods in their approach to the subject matter. Stanislavsky encouraged actors to draw their performances from the subtext of the story.

Despite the film's limited release and subsequent negative reviews, together with the fact that Argento was used to making films on a somewhat grander scale, the director maintained that it was a good experience, and he received nothing but support and encouragement from his American crew.

Comments

While Edgar Allan Poe was a major influence on the work of Argento, the director had never directly adapted any of Poe's work before *Two Evil Eyes*. The early nineties was a popular time for Poe adaptations, as Stuart Gordon and Roger Corman proved with their takes on *The Pit and the Pendulum* (1991) and *The Masque of the Red Death* (1990) respectively.

The film opens with images of Poe's hometown of Baltimore, including a shot of his grave. Argento had apparently filmed quite a lengthy segment about the life and work of Poe as a prelude to the two films he and Romero made, but it was considered too long by the distributors and only a few shots remain in the completed film. There was also supposed to be a framing device around the two films, with 'Poe' himself relaying the tales of terror, but this was also scrapped.

Argento's segment *The Black Cat* is loosely based on the titular short story by Poe, but the director also pays homage to many of the troubled writer's other tales of the macabre. Amongst the array of Poe allusions on display in Argento's love letter to the writer are references to *The Pit and the Pendulum, Berenice, Annabel Lee, Ligeia, The Tell Tale Heart, The Premature Burial, The Fall of the House of Usher* and *The Narrative of Gordon Pym*.

Romero had initially wanted to adapt *The Masque of the Red Death*, but changed his mind when he realised that Roger Corman was remaking his own version.

Romero decided instead to adapt *The Facts in the Case of M Valdemar*, a dark morality tale featuring the living dead and revenge from beyond the grave. The two segments of the film differ as much as the directors who helmed them; Romero is a solid storyteller who has a practical, no-frills approach to his subject matter, and meticulously planned his shoot, whereas Argento prefers to revel in style and provocative trimmings, taking his usual experimental approach to its abstract conclusion.

Style/Technical

Two Evil Eyes has a different look and style from many of Argento's other films. The hyper-realistic photography by Beppe Maccari lacks the striking results of Argento's previous work, and the film is the closest the director has come to creating something that could be described as 'conventional'. The camerawork, however, is as ravishing

Disturbing revelations for the amateur sleuths in *The Bird with the Crystal Plumage*

Another victim is slashed to ribbons in *The Bird with the Crystal Plumage*

Casoni falls to his death in the shattering climax of *Cat O'Nine Tails*

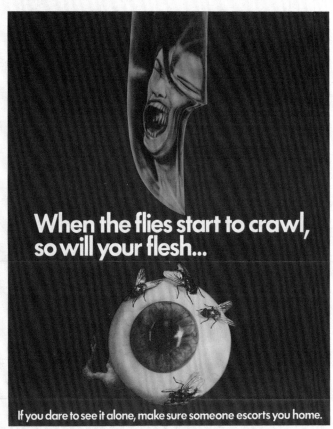

When the flies start to crawl, so will your flesh...

If you dare to see it alone, make sure someone escorts you home.

Paramount Pictures presents
A film directed by Dario Argento

"Four Flies on Grey Velvet"

with Michael Brandon Mimsy Farmer Jean Pierre Marielle Francine Racette and Bud Spencer

Music scored by Ennio Morricone   Produced by Salvatore Argento   Seda Spettacoli – Rome and Universal Prod. France-Paris

Technicolor® – Techniscope®   A Paramount Picture

PG

72/331

Creating a buzz: promotional artwork for *Four Flies on Grey Velvet*, the final film in Argento's 'Animal Trilogy'

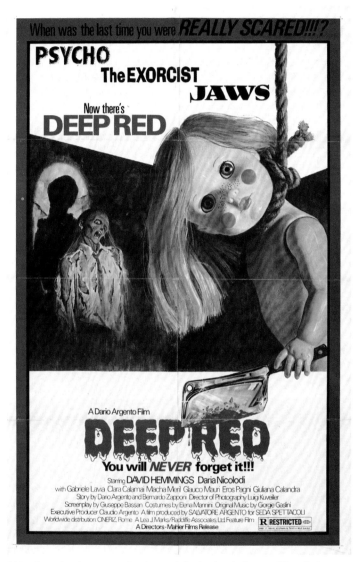

A bloody masterpiece: promotional artwork for the deeply deranged *Deep Red*

Pat's extravagant execution marks the first of many in Argento's luridly coloured, ear-splitting classic, *Suspiria*

The diabolical Miss Tanner severely reprimands Daniel in a scene from *Suspiria*

Seeing Red: Suzy suspects something sinister is afoot in *Suspiria*

Gothic chic: darkly beautiful promotional artwork for *Inferno*

'I love you. I love you all.' Promotional artwork for Argento's paranormal fairytale, *Phenomena*

Sadistic gaze: A still from *Opera* provides one of Argento's most disturbing and enduring images

More shocking sights and eye-violation in the deliriously violent *Mother of Tears*

Mater Lachrymarum revels in the suffering of one of her many victims in *Mother of Tears*

Another victim folds in *The Card Player*

She's not bluffing: Anna Mari reveals her poker face in *The Card Player*

Promotional artwork for Argento's blood-spattered *Giallo*

as ever. Argento was keen to convey events as much as possible from the fiendish cat's point of view, and the beautiful Steadicam shots by Terry Gilliam regular Nicola Pecorini really deliver, creating some impressive images with a handheld 35mm camera that stalks the characters from ground level, darting around and over furniture. Initially Argento wanted to use an anamorphic lens to enhance the cat's-eye point-of-view shots, creating a vertical lens instead of a round one, but decided against this in the end.

Early on in the film, when Rod arrives at the first murder scene and sets the pendulum in motion, Argento's camera swoops down on, and then through, the split-in-two corpse splayed out on the table, creating a dizzying and macabre effect.

Argento was deeply inspired by the urban landscapes of American cities, a visual motif that would also seep into *Trauma*, lending both films a grittier edge.

The film's make-up and special effects were designed by Tom Savini and, amongst other gory delights, he created a litter of monstrous mechanical kittens and a double of Harvey Keitel's head, to feature in the scene where he is impaled with a stake that erupts out of his mouth. Keitel was apparently so grossed out by the thought of this that he had his attorney ensure the head would never appear on set while he was working, as he might have been 'freaked out' by it.

Savini and Argento bonded over their grisly work in *Two Evil Eyes*, the language barrier not interfering with their mutual enthusiasm for gory effects.

The murder of Annabel is particularly graphic, and Argento films it through a sheen of melancholy as she fixes her gaze on the audience, who are viewing the bloody actions from Rod's point of view, thrusting her hands up in an effort to protect herself from his cleaver.

The Black Cat is tightly plotted, more so than anything Argento had directed before, and the restraint he demonstrates results in a fairly diluted film, stripped of the usual baroque flamboyance associated with the maestro's work.

Argento does find time to slip in a few references to artworks that complement the dark themes running through the story. For example, when Rod lays Annabel's body in the bath, the image recalls Millais' 'Ophelia', hinting at the melancholic beauty found in death.

Themes

Rod Usher is quite a typical Argento protagonist in that he works in the world of art as a photographer. He is also an archetypal Poe character, incapable of escaping from his past or from the destiny he is hurtling towards. Like Peter Neal in *Tenebrae* and the two protagonists in *Trauma*, Rod has a troubled mind from the outset. Something of a departure for Argento, *Two Evil Eyes* makes no attempt to mask the killer at its heart.

Rod is also an unusual protagonist in that he harbours none of the repressed traumatic experiences of other Argento murderers. He has no psychosexual anxiety at his core, nor is he killing to keep a dark secret from rippling to the surface; he simply kills because he is interested in exploring the darker side of his own nature.

In the opening slice of narration, he pointedly asks the audience if they have ever felt compelled to do something simply because they knew it was forbidden. Poe addresses this very question in his essay 'Imp of the Perverse', detailing his belief that every person has a dark side and the potential to do evil and despicable things, a theme Hitchcock also explored in his work, most notably *Rope* (1948).

Rod's occupation serves to highlight Argento's themes of voyeurism, spectatorship, 'the image' and 'looking'. As a photographer, images are important to him, specifically images depicting the darker side of human nature. Through his camera, rather like Argento, and by extension the audience, Rod interacts with death from a safe distance. At various times during the film, though, he becomes more proactive in his interactions; he switches on the pendulum and he strangles the cat. By the time he murders Annabel he is no longer viewing atrocities through the distancing and protective lens of a camera, but full on through his own eyes.

Various shots throughout the film combine to reinforce Argento's preoccupation with the act of 'looking': shots from the cat's point of view as it stalks Rod, Rod spying on Annabel with her student, and Mr Pym peering through the peephole of the Ushers' front door.

The aesthetics of death that Rod seems obsessed with capturing on film recall Argento's own preoccupation with aestheticised murders.

The brief allusion to 'Ophelia' highlights the notion of 'idyllic death', a concept Poe himself reflected on in his 'Philosophy of Composition', which led him to the conclusion that the most poetical topic in the world was the death of a beautiful woman.

The photographs Rod takes in order to compile his book are in a similar vein to the work of Arthur Fellig, a photojournalist famous for his stark black-and-white images, capturing urban grotesqueness and crime.

Music

Brian De Palma's regular scorer, Pino Donaggio, provides a suitably frantic score here, with more than its fair share of nods to Bernard Herrmann's *Psycho* riff. At times it resembles a deranged carousel theme and the use of a shrill string section perfectly complements Rod Usher's unhinged state of mind and eventual mental collapse.

Verdict

Argento films the escalating frenzy of events with his usual style and precision, while Romero quietly ponders death in a creepy but stagnant tale of revenge from beyond the grave. As a result, *Two Evil Eyes* is a very disjointed and uneven piece of work from two filmmakers who are as competent and individual in their approach to their craft as they are different from each other. An intriguing footnote in the careers of both men.

Trauma (1993)

Directed/Written/Produced by: Dario Argento
Co-written by: TED Kline
Music by: Pino Donaggio
Cinematography: Raffaele Mertes
Edited by: Bennett Goldberg
Production Designer: Billy Jet
Special Effects: Tom Savini
Cast: Christopher Rydell (David Parsons), Asia Argento (Aura Petrescu), Frederic Forrest (Dr Leopold Judd), Piper Laurie (Adriana Petrescu), James Russo (Captain Travis), Laura Johnson (Grace Harrington), Brad Dourif (Dr Lloyd)

Synopsis

Anorexic teen runaway Aura is stopped from throwing herself off a bridge by David Parsons, a young graphic artist. She has just escaped from a psychiatric clinic and David feels obliged to help her. She is soon apprehended by two men from the clinic who bring her home. That night she witnesses the beheadings of her parents by an unseen assailant who garrottes victims when it rains. Seeking out David again, Aura begs him to help her find out who killed her parents and stop them killing anyone else.

Background

Still keen to crack the American market after the commercial failure of *Two Evil Eyes*, Argento teamed up with US horror writer, editor of *Twilight Zone* magazine and novelist TED Klein to pen this morbid tale of revenge and psychosis. Possible titles considered for the project included *Moving Guillotine* and *Aura's Enigma* before Argento finally decided on the somewhat more appropriate *Trauma*. The film cost $7 million and was shot in Minneapolis in August and September 1992.

Argento allegedly lifted personal experiences from his own life and placed them in the film in a more pronounced manner. The director struggled with an eating disorder in his youth, as did his stepdaughter, Anna (Nicolodi's other daughter from a previous relationship). Argento also claims that when he saw a young woman being sick on a busy street in the States and no one helping her, he was so troubled that he had to address the experience through his work in order to exorcise it from his mind.

Argento had a difficult time in casting *Trauma*. He offered the lead role to his daughter Asia, and this marked the first time he would direct her. The choice generated accusations of nepotism. Asia defended his decision, retorting that she didn't believe her father would have cast her if he didn't think she was capable of portraying the character. She allegedly based her performance on that of her mother in Mario Bava's last film, *Shock* (1977).

The role of David was offered to James Spader, Tim Roth and John Cusack, but all three were seemingly worried about portraying a character who would return to drugs in a time of crisis. Chris Rydell jumped at the chance to work with Argento and savoured the difficult role. Avid Argento fan Bridget Fonda was apparently offered the role of Grace, but declined due to creative differences.

Despite the huge amount of respect Piper Laurie and Frederic Forrest had for Argento as a director, they apparently spent the majority of filming laughing at the absurdity of the script.

Comments

Argento described *Trauma* as 'Deep Soul. My *Deep Red* for a new generation.'

Although Argento was accused of 'Americanising' this film, he still retained his European sensibilities, proving uncomfortable with executives in the US who marketed the film as 'a horror film if David Lynch directed one'. This highlights the difficulty the American market had in trying to find a niche for Argento.

Trauma was greeted with even more derision than *Two Evil Eyes*, with critics and fans of Argento claiming the director had sold out to

America with his latest, watered-down offering. Despite this alleged dilution of *Trauma*, the film did not escape the censors in the States, with one notable scene being trimmed: when Brad Dourif is decapitated in the lift shaft (recalling Martha's fate in *Deep Red*), his head falls down the shaft and is impaled on a spike at the bottom. The fate of his head is lifted completely from the finished film.

This is another example of an Argento film falling prey to rabid censorship – *Tenebrae* and *Phenomena* were released in the States in severely edited forms and re-titled *Unsane* and *Creepers* respectively. Working outside of Italy meant he would again have to compromise his vision and lose complete control over his film.

Trauma, like so many of Argento's other films, consists of a series of astounding set pieces such as the séance, echoing the creepy séance in *Deep Red*, and the hospital scenes; indeed, all of the death scenes unfold like miniature movies themselves.

Style/Technical

Argento believed at one stage that *Trauma* was his darkest film to date. He intended all of the shots to convey something subtextual and stated that all of the interior scenes represented the human body and the warped psyches of the characters. It is a purposefully cold, dark and gloomy film. The exteriors are shot with more warmth, however, as Argento bathes proceedings in sun-hued, burnished yellows and deep blues.

The director had considered shooting the film in Pittsburgh, but *The Silence of the Lambs* (1991) had already taken advantage of that location, hence the final choice of Minneapolis.

The colour scheme of *Trauma* evokes the palette used in Domenico Beccafumi's famous painting of St Catherine of Siena, a muted, washed-out mixture of browns, ambers, whites and pale blues.

Trauma's cinematographer Raffaele Mertes, who also photographed *The Sect*, was asked by Argento to devise a film-noir look with 'elements of fantasy' for *Trauma*. Mertes utilised a special printing process called EMR that washes down the colours in the film, creating an almost monochromatic look. This film really marks the beginning of Argento's move into a more realist approach to the look of his films, as evident in his subsequent works *The Stendhal Syndrome*, *Sleepless*, *The Card Player* and *Do You Like Hitchcock?*, and the film's muted tones predate the likes of *Se7en* (1995) and *8MM* (1999), with all the rain and water imagery conjuring up Argento's own *Inferno*.

Argento specifically created scenes to use the latest technology, such as the micro-Louma crane used to convey events from a manic butterfly's perspective as it is chased around the garden by a young boy. These seemingly spontaneous Steadicam shots were lensed by Kirk Gardener.

Production designer Billy Jet built many of the sets raised off the ground so Argento could manoeuvre the camera around them and film events to curious effect. *Trauma* contains considerably fewer violent scenes than most of Argento's other work. The director was hoping to create more suspense by only implying the violence in a 'Lewton-esque' manner, with quick editing and extreme close-ups.

Special effects were once again created by Tom Savini and it was wise of Argento not to show the decapitated heads in gruesome detail, as they reveal some of Savini's most shoddy and unconvincing work. Indeed, the film is so bloodless that it received an 'unrestricted' rating in Italy, the same rating usually applied to family-orientated movies.

Themes

Trauma, like *Phenomena*, unfolds as a compilation of themes that recur throughout Argento's oeuvre. Aura, despite her flaws and instability, is still portrayed as a strong character. She is also a marked outsider because of her psychological problems and the fact that she and her parents are Romanian immigrants living in America. Both she and David are also outsiders due to their dark and troubled pasts, and the characterisation afforded them in the film is not evident in many of Argento's other leading characters. Despite the claims that Argento sold out with *Trauma*, he still manages to be subversive in having an ex-junkie and an anorexic as his protagonists.

The casting of his daughter Asia has inspired critics to suggest that, in this way, Argento is reliving his experiences working with Daria Nicolodi. The characters that Asia would portray, like her mother, would not escape unscathed in Argento's films... The scenes in *Trauma* and *Tenebrae* where Aura and Anna, respectively, are screaming in the rain are uncannily similar.

Like many Argento protagonists, and typical of Argento's own brand of *gialli*, Aura witnesses a terrible event (like Sam in *The Bird with the Crystal Plumage*, Marc in *Deep Red*, Gianni in *Tenebrae* and Betty in *Opera*) and has to try and recall what she saw/misidentified in order to discover the identity of the killer.

Argento again seems to go out of his way to deliberately hide the identity of the killer. When Aura witnesses her father's murder, the killer's identity is concealed using a sleight-of-hand visual trick.

There are a few clues peppered throughout the film but, again, like most of the investigations carried out by Argento's sleuths, the revelation of the killer's identity is arrived at via a more abstract approach than the usual logical deduction.

The film is overflowing with red herrings, notably the very odd Dr Judd, who is revealed to be Adriana's lover and has been attempting to conceal her crimes by framing himself as the killer.

While the black leather gloves of the killer are present, gone are the phallic knives and blades; in their place is a handheld mechanical garrotte (dubbed the 'noose-o-matic' by its creator Tom Savini).

In *Trauma*, Argento doesn't actually show us the catalyst for the surfacing of Adriana's repressed traumatic memory. Savini was initially to play a construction worker accidentally decapitated, inadvertently stirring Adriana's dormant memories of her appalling past experience. However, this scene was never filmed.

Like Martha in *Deep Red*, Adriana needs to recreate elements from the initial traumatic event. While Martha replays the lullaby just before she kills, Adriana kills only when it rains; and when it doesn't rain, like in the scene where she kills the nurse in the motel, she sets off the sprinkler system creating artificial rain.

Again referencing Domenico Beccafumi's 'St Catherine of Siena' in the scene where Aura binds her breasts, Argento seems to be drawing parallels between the historical figure depicted in this painting and the character of Aura, a somewhat troubled young woman dedicating her life to achieving one goal. The scene has connotations of self-flagellation and dogmatic determination.

As in *Two Evil Eyes*, Argento references Millais' 'Ophelia' in the implied watery fate of Aura. A few days later, David passes by a gallery, sees a copy of this painting in the window and becomes deeply affected by it (a hint of things to come in *The Stendhal Syndrome*).

Argento nods to *Rear Window* (1954) and *Psycho* (1960) in a couple of knowing shots involving a shower and a nosy kid with binoculars.

Freudian psychoanalysis finds its way back into Argento's work with a vengeance in *Trauma*. David's colleague defines anorexia in Freudian terms, fixing on the psychosexual subtext of the disease as Freud himself saw it.

In early drafts of the script, the killer was obsessed with the French Revolution; hence the inclusion of a child's cut-out paper theatre depicting a beheading in the film's opening shot. The use of children's toys and their sometimes sinister connotations mirrors similar shots in *Deep Red* (and indeed Mario Bava's *Kill Baby Kill* [1966], where a bouncing ball has rarely seemed so menacing). This fascination with the French Revolution also finds its way into the film in the form of the severed heads still able to whisper their final words after being disembodied. Legend has it that the severed head of Marie Antoinette uttered a few words from the basket beneath the guillotine. The paper theatre is later glimpsed sitting by Nicholas's crib when David staggers through dizzying drapes and net curtains to discover the dark secret in Adriana's house, crossing over a threshold that will change him forever.

Adriana's sinister house and the creepy goings-on in it recall the sinister abodes of *Deep Red*, *Phenomena*, the 'Three Mothers' trilogy and *The Church*.

The method of death deployed to dispatch the killer in *Trauma*, and also in *Deep Red* and *Four Flies on Grey Velvet*, is decapitation. Interestingly, in *The Sect* one character discusses the concept of the human soul inhabiting the head. This idea is reiterated in *Trauma*; the subsequent removal of Adriana's head, laying to rest the troubled soul within, is therefore a thematically fitting dénouement. Freud's influence is also evident in this idea, as he viewed the removal of the head as an act of castration.

Trauma marks the return of Argento's monstrous maternal figure in the formidable form of Adriana Petrescu. The latest in a long line of female killers in Argento's work, she rekindles memories of Monica in *The Bird with the Crystal Plumage*, Nina in *Four Flies on Grey Velvet*, Martha in *Deep Red*, the Three Mothers from *Suspiria*, *Inferno*, and *Mother of Tears*, Frau Brückner in *Phenomena*, Betty's sadistic mother in *Opera* and Yellow's cruel and selfish mother in *Giallo*.

Music

Pino Donaggio's eclectic score for *Trauma* is a rather uneven and ultimately nondescript affair. At times it resembles a second-rate Bernard Herrmann score. Blasting brass and shrieking strings are abundant, but they fail to create any memorable atmosphere. One stroke of genius, however, is the haunting and ethereal track 'Ruby Rain', which echoes fleetingly throughout the film before being used to full effect in the scene where David plunges into the lake at night searching for Aura. His only light is that of the moon, and the whole scene is bathed in an eerie, yet beautiful quality. The moody strains of this song are utilised to startling effect, rather like the use of This Mortal Coil's 'Song to the Siren' in David Lynch's *Lost Highway* (1997).

Trivia

Before deciding to film in Minneapolis, Argento stayed in Pittsburgh scouting locations for *Trauma*. He was invited by Tom Savini and John Landis to make a cameo appearance as a sinister ambulance driver in Landis's *Innocent Blood* (1992).

Verdict

Trauma is not as bad as it has been made out to be in the past. Yes, it lacks many of the things that Argento's fans have come to hold in high regard, but it does contain many elements usually associated with his work. The film marks an interesting point in Argento's career and proves that he is a visionary director constantly experimenting and pushing forward. *Trauma* might not be the '*Deep Red* for a new generation' that Argento wanted it to be, but it is a thoroughly entertaining and solid entry in his canon of work nonetheless.

AESTHETICS OF BLOOD

After the poor returns of *Two Evil Eyes*, prompting its co-producer Achille Manzotti to sue Argento's production company ADC for losses, and the scathing reviews *Trauma* garnered, Argento returned home to Italy exhausted, disheartened and determined never to work with a major studio again. He reluctantly realised that his dark and disturbing visions were perhaps too progressive for American audiences. Holding high his middle finger to critics, he set about work on his next film, which would see him return to form and unleash some of his most controversial and disturbing imagery to date.

La sindrome di Stendhal/The Stendhal Syndrome (1996)

'Works of art have power over us.
Great works of art have great power.'

Directed/Written/Produced by: Dario Argento
Produced by: Giuseppe Colombo
Music by: Ennio Morricone
Cinematography: Giuseppe Rotunno
Edited by: Angelo Nicolini
Production Designer: Antonello Geleng
Special Effects: Sergio Stivaletti
Cast: Asia Argento (Anna Manni), Thomas Kretschmann (Alfredo Grossi), Marco Leonardi (Marco Longhi), Luigi Diberti (Chief Inspector Manetti), Julien Lambroschini (Marie Bale), Paolo Bonacelli (Dr Cavanna)

Synopsis

Visiting the Uffizi Gallery following an anonymous tip-off that the serial killer and rapist she is pursuing will be there, Detective Anna Manni is seemingly struck by the Stendhal Syndrome and overcome by the many works of art around her. Fainting, she imagines she has entered one of the paintings. A handsome stranger called Alfredo helps her back to her hotel where he reveals himself to be the killer she is after. He rapes and kidnaps her and uses her disorder against her. Her traumatic experience begins to unlock another side of her personality as she struggles to maintain control and stop Alfredo once and for all.

Background

When planning the film that would eventually become *The Stendhal Syndrome*, Argento had thought of remaking *The Golem* (1920). However, once he came across the titular syndrome in a medical book, his interest was aroused. Stendhal was the penname of French writer Marie-Henri Beyle, author of *The Red and the Black* (1830). While Beyle was visiting museums in Florence he was affected physically and psychologically by the works of art on display. The syndrome named after him is a form of mental collapse that manifests itself physically when an individual views powerful works of art. It has been known to cause split personalities, self-mutilation and hallucinations. Many tourists still visiting Florence today are known to be affected by the syndrome. In fact, several beds in local hospitals are always reserved for such cases!

This was the first Italian film to use CGI and Argento is still the only filmmaker ever granted permission to shoot in the prestigious Uffizi Museum, a gesture that highlights the high regard the director is held in by Italians. Shooting took place in July 1995 in Florence and Rome. Initial plans for *The Stendhal Syndrome* included filming it in Arizona with Bridget Fonda in the lead role, but Argento had had enough of America and wanted to return to his roots. Securing funding from Medusa Distribution, Argento set out to make a shocking and explicit film that would silence his critics and woo his fans.

Comments

The Stendhal Syndrome in many ways marked a return home for Argento. With it he returned to form and once again was completely in control of his work, answering to no one. The result is probably one of his most intense and unsettling films ever. Argento lovingly photographs Florence and Rome and, in the scene where Anna and Marie are driving through Rome, Marie is shouting out the names of Italian artists in a celebration of Italian culture. This seems deliberate on Argento's part; he is returning to his own rich culture and mining it for inspiration after the scorn heaped on *Trauma* and the accusations levelled against him of selling out.

While the film was heavily criticised on its release, it is now undergoing something of a critical reappraisal and has a strong cult following. The film seems to be a response to those who dismissed *Two Evil Eyes* and *Trauma* for being too conventional and commercial, and the shocking and provocative imagery on display in this devastatingly brutal film ensures that audiences know Argento is back with a vengeance. The director himself commented that *The Stendhal Syndrome* was 'the most brutal' film he had made.

He came under much criticism for casting his own daughter in such a controversial role. Asia defended him, however, claiming that she was attracted to the role as she felt it would challenge her in a way that many other roles couldn't. She has noted on a number of occasions that she has a deep respect for her father's daring film work and, because of their relationship, feels that he can guide her and draw out a memorable performance.

Thomas Kretschmann plays Alfredo as a deranged monster with no redeeming qualities. The actor practised rolling a real razor blade around in his mouth for the infamous scene where Alfredo produces a razor blade from his mouth and slashes Anna's face with it. Kretschmann improvised quite a lot and Argento was accommodating of this; a notable improvisation appears when Alfredo simulates oral sex with a gun.

Argento flaunts the affects of art on individuals in a way that seems to mirror the charges against his own films and the negative effects they have been accused of inflicting on individuals.

At times, the film resembles a typical rape-revenge narrative and, interestingly, Asia Argento watched Abel Ferrara's *Ms 45* (1981) for inspiration. There seem to be two narratives running throughout the film: Anna discovering her ailment in her grisly encounters with Alfredo and then Anna dealing with her inner turmoil and emerging schizophrenia, her Stendhal Syndrome relegated to the background. Strangely for Argento, he emphasises the psychological effects of violence on Anna as well as depicting the actual violence.

Style/Technical

Continuing on from the subtle palette of *Trauma*, Argento imbues this film with a calmer look that belies the brutal acts of violence lurking within it. The muted tones created by cinematographer Giuseppe Rotunno don't hinder or detract from the appearance of the various works of art depicted.

Even though *The Stendhal Syndrome* was the first ever Italian film to use CGI, Argento doesn't overuse it. Obviously, compared with today's standards, some of it looks decidedly clumsy. However, there are a few flashes of brilliance when it is used with restraint, as in the scene where Anna steps into her own memory through a Rembrandt painting in her hotel room; the painting dissolves to black and drips away, creating a dark entrance to her unfolding memory. Through these experiments with CGI, Argento is able to show us even more gory and exquisite details; we follow pills that Anna has swallowed down her throat into her stomach and we follow a bullet as it blasts from a gun, catching Alfredo's reflection as it goes.

The violence on display in *The Stendhal Syndrome* is not the usual highly stylised violence one would associate with the director. It is raw and abrasive and all the more disturbing because of this. Argento also depicts rape for the first time in this work. Though several scenes in his previous films hint at a sexual element to the crimes, such as the bedroom murder in *The Bird with the Crystal Plumage* when the killer strokes the victim's leg with a knife, he has never portrayed the actual act before. Even the sensual victims and overtly sexual flashbacks in *Tenebrae* convey sexual undertones through metaphor. The violence in this film, however, is grimy, intense and very real.

Once again we see events from the killer's point of view: we stalk Marie through the room full of sculptures before his death in the museum; we offer a woman a rose and then lure her down a side-street to rape and eventually murder her. All this is shown in graphic detail from the assailant's point of view and therefore ours too. Voyeurism is also presented to us as detached spectatorship, evident in the scene where Anna is fleeing from Alfredo. This is witnessed by several people looking out of their windows, but they do nothing to help her, reminiscent of the tramp who witnesses the murder of the shoplifter in *Tenebrae*.

In the scene where Alfredo shoots a woman in the face, Argento deploys similar techniques to those used in *Four Flies on Grey Velvet* and *Opera*, where the camera follows the bullet as it passes through the woman's face and out the other side, leaving a gaping hole that Alfredo peers through menacingly.

The film's many hallucinations prompted by works of art provide the surreal and nightmarish imagery we've come to expect from Argento. The first of these is when Anna views 'The Fall of Icarus' by Brueghel and imagines herself under the ocean in the painting, kissing a 'Bosch-esque' fish with a strangely ethereal face.

The production design of the lair where Alfredo abuses Anna is extremely unsettling. Five artists took two days to create the grimy and depraved graffiti that stains the walls of this location. Production designer Antonello Geleng also designed the sets in *The Sect*.

Themes

Argento has often used art as a tool for destruction in his work: the huge sculpture that traps Sam and the painting that causes Monica's deadly psychosis in *The Bird with the Crystal Plumage*; the crystal ornament Suzy uses to stab the Mother of Sighs in *Suspiria*; the spiky sculpture that impales Peter in *Tenebrae*; and the ornate obelisk that impales Mater Lachrymarum in *Mother of Tears*. The director has always been fascinated by the subversive nature of art, typically believed to raise the spirit, not crush it or take it over. Argento considers his films as art and, as such, it can be said that, once again, he is exploring the concept of violence in cinema and its alleged affect on viewers.

With *The Stendhal Syndrome*, Argento takes this connection between art and death to its cruel and logical conclusion, aligning it with murder as a highly cathartic act that temporarily banishes the demons from within. Connotations of the 'tortured artist' are rife throughout the film, particularly in the scene depicting Anna covering herself in paint and curling up on top of her canvas. She essentially uses her own body as a canvas, redesigning herself through the various guises she adopts and her self-mutilation. Art is everywhere in *The Stendhal Syndrome*, from the imposing statues lining the streets of Florence in the opening shots to the crude and base imagery of the lurid graffiti adorning the walls of Alfredo's lair. Interestingly, Anna's various paintings and artworks throughout the film were all created and provided by Asia herself.

Argento uses specific pieces of art to highlight themes running through the film. For example, he includes shots of 'Birth of Venus' and 'Primavera' by Botticelli and Caravaggio's 'Medusa' (Freud cited Medusa as an example of the female castrator and, indeed, female castration), which are all constructs of women ranging from the 'virtuous' to the 'monstrous' – all stages Anna traverses on her traumatic journey. The artists are all men and these paintings represent their impressions of 'woman'.

There is no explanation for Alfredo's unhinged mental state – no secrets to unlock. He is simply presented to us as a monster.

Psychological transfer is a major theme in this film as in the director's previous *gialli*. What's different about *The Stendhal Syndrome* is that it unfolds as Argento's first film to focus on an in-depth character study and the subsequent mental breakdown of a woman undergoing traumatic events. Usually, such attention to plot specifics and the psychological effects of violence is secondary to striking visuals and only revealed at the climax, as in Monica's psychological transfer in *The Bird with the Crystal Plumage*, Nina in *Four Flies on Grey Velvet* and Peter Neal in *Tenebrae*.

The shot in *Tenebrae* where Inspector Germani stoops out of frame to reveal Neal standing directly behind him is mirrored in this film when Anna gets into a taxi and rolls up her window so Alfredo's image is reflected on it and imposed over her own face.

As in previous films such as *The Bird with the Crystal Plumage*, *Four Flies on Grey Velvet*, *Deep Red* and *Tenebrae*, Argento subverts notions of gender to dizzying effect: Marie, the young man Anna falls for, has a feminine name; Anna makes herself look like a boy to desexualise herself; she simulates raping her boyfriend Marco and is domineering with Marie; Alfredo adopts a female voice to lure Anna to the museum; the desexualised Anna adopts an overtly feminine persona after her second encounter with Alfredo, donning a blonde wig. Anna alternates between masculine and feminine guises over the course of the film, as a way of dealing with her trauma. It would appear that Argento is intent on disturbing and disorienting the audience as much as he is Anna. Perhaps most interestingly, *The Stendhal Syndrome* has a male and a female killer, both killing because the other drove them to it.

Men and women have often caused each other to kill in Argento's films: the female killers of *The Bird with the Crystal Plumage, Four Flies on Grey Velvet* and *Deep Red* were all driven to murder by men; the male killers in *Tenebrae, Opera* and *Jenifer* were driven to murder by women.

Hitchcockian themes are resurrected with aplomb in *The Stendhal Syndrome* – the violence stemming from sexual perversion mirrors that of *Psycho* (1960) and *Frenzy* (1972); the film's trajectory follows the mental unravelling of a woman's mind as in *Marnie* (1964) and *Suspicion* (1941); and the protagonist suffers from a severe psychological impairment similar to that in *Vertigo* (1958).

Knives are not used as much as they have been in previous Argento films; instead we have guns, a more brutal, masculine weapon. Alfredo usually shoots his victims at the point of orgasm, enhancing the 'phallic' connotations associated with guns. When Alfredo steals Anna's gun at the beginning of the film, his actions can be viewed as a way of 'castrating' her.

While Anna's mother is absent from the film's narrative, she appears in a flashback when she takes a young Anna to look at an art gallery. This is the first time Anna succumbs to the syndrome and it is mentioned that Anna's mother was an artist. Although she is not directly responsible for Anna's ailment, her part in it is implied. She provides another example, albeit a more subtle one, of Argento's sinister maternal figures.

The notion of water as a nurturing element is again subverted by Argento and, as in *Inferno*, water takes on a threatening role here too. When Anna steps into the painting of a waterfall, it foreshadows the watery death she will bestow upon Alfredo and the river that will consume his body, denying her the satisfaction of knowing he is really dead.

Music

Argento and Ennio Morricone resolved the differences that had come to a head on *Four Flies on Grey Velvet*, and Morricone provides a haunting and beautifully dark score for *The Stendhal Syndrome*, submerging everything under sinister strings, eerily seductive vocal arrangements and cacophonous, paranoia-inducing whispers.

Trivia

Co-writer Franco Ferrini wanted the film to end with Anna imprisoned, her only source of consolation a print of one of Gainsborough's pastoral landscapes that she eventually escapes into.

Verdict

After the notable failure of *Two Evil Eyes* and *Trauma*, Argento proves he is still a master of the macabre and capable of disturbing and shocking audiences. *The Stendhal Syndrome* is a deeply unsettling work from a director who has consistently proved that he is still a unique figure in cinema. You will never again feel safe in an art gallery.

Il fantasma dell'opera/The Phantom of the Opera (1998)

Directed/Written by: Dario Argento
Co-written by: Gérard Brach
Produced by: Claudio Argento & Giuseppe Colombo
Music by: Ennio Morricone
Cinematography: Ronnie Taylor BSC
Edited by: Anna Rosa Napoli AMC
Production Designer: Antonello Geleng
Special Effects: Sergio Stivaletti
Cast: Julian Sands (The Phantom), Asia Argento (Christine Daaé), Andrea Di Stefano (Baron Raoul De Chagny), Coralina Cataldi-Tassoni (Honorine), Nadia Rinaldi (Carlotta Altieri), David D'Ingeo (Alfred), Kitty Kéri (Paulette)

Synopsis

An abandoned baby boy in a basket is retrieved from an underground river by a group of rats. He grows up in the catacombs beneath the

Paris opera house and falls in love with a young opera singer named Christine Daaé. They appear to share a telepathic link and, in his determination to make her a star and claim her as his lover, he pursues a bloody quest to rid himself of anyone who stands in his way.

Background

Phantom of the Opera is Dario Argento's most expensive film to date and its inception came about as a result of a survey conducted by Medusa, Argento's film distributor. The survey revealed that filmgoers most wanted to see a remake of *Phantom of the Opera* directed by Argento. When the director was presented with these findings he leapt at the chance to film his own take on one of his favourite films.

After initial plans to shoot in Russia, with a backdrop of the 1917 Revolution, *Phantom of the Opera* was filmed on location in Hungary during January 1998. Much of the film was shot within custom-built sets located in Budapest and in the opera house designed by Charles Garnier, whose Paris opera house inspired Gaston Leroux to write *The Phantom of the Opera* in 1910. Argento had already produced *The Church* in Hungary and had fallen in love with the country.

Argento co-wrote the script with Gerard Brach who wrote *The Fearless Vampire Killers* (1967) for Roman Polanski. Brach suffers from acute agoraphobia and is a recluse. Argento visited him in his flat in Paris and the two worked steadily, pausing only to devour the meals sent up from the restaurant below.

Comments

Those who lambasted *Phenomena*, and indeed *Trauma*, as the nadir of Argento's career hadn't seen anything yet. *Phantom of the Opera* is an absolute mess of a film. In trying to combine too many different elements, such as horror, romance, comedy and stark violence against the backdrop of early twentieth-century Paris, the film is rendered uneven and overwrought. Argento at this stage believed that the only way he could genuinely shock his audiences was to do the unthinkable and present them with a film dabbling in romance and humour. The result is indeed shocking, but certainly not in the way the director intended.

Argento constantly strives to go against the grain and *Phantom of the Opera* was released into cinemas at a time when *Scream* (1996) and other teen-orientated, postmodern slasher films were at the height of their popularity. While the film is indeed a refined and sensual affair compared to other genre films of the time, outside of Italy it went largely unnoticed and straight to video.

Argento also defied expectations in his somewhat misguided representation of the Phantom. Wisely taking his daughter's advice and not creating a Phantom that was a grotesque hybrid of man and rat (complete with rodent teeth), the director created a monster in the guise of a handsome man, his appearance belying the evil and twisted mind within. There is no equivalent 'unmasking' scene to reveal the humanity behind the monster as in the original film – a moment that, while unnerving, was charged with an undeniable pathos. Instead, Argento subverts this notion and all we are left with is the less interesting vampish guy who is actually a monster. Merchant Ivory regular Julian Sands plays the Phantom as a seemingly misunderstood and tortured artist; however, as the film progresses it becomes evident that he is insane.

Asia portrays Christine as a strong woman, perhaps imbuing a little too much of her own strength and determination into her character, a trait that adds to the postmodern slant. The actress also took singing lessons and, though it isn't her voice we hear when Christine sings, Asia provides all of the gestures and movements associated with opera singers.

Style/Technical

Phantom of the Opera is exquisitely filmed and great attention is heaped onto the period detail. The production design is flawless and there are several set pieces within the film that are visually stunning. The Phantom's lair, for example, is brimming with faded opulence and decadence, furnished with salvaged items from the glorious building above. There is an impressive shot at the beginning of the film when the camera moves through the catacombs, up through the layers of earth denoting the years that have passed since the infant Phantom was abandoned, and emerges outside the opera house to follow some of the patrons inside.

Argento seems to have been particularly inspired by the work of painter Georges de la Tour, whose use of light and reflection is recreated by Argento to breathtaking effect throughout the film. The scene in which Christine sits in front of a mirror, holding her hand in front of a candle, is a replica of 'La Madeleine aux deux Flammes' by de la Tour. The pink glow of her hand and the veins backlit within it as she holds it in front of the candle is an intimate and beautiful sight. Argento utilises lighting that appears natural: candles, lanterns and fires are abundant throughout the picture.

Argento references the work of Bosch and Degas. Indeed, Degas is depicted in a few scenes painting the young ballet dancers. When the Phantom is dreaming of the humanoid creatures caught in a giant rat trap, the image that appears before us is a Bosch-inspired orgy of bird-headed people writhing in agony, much like the pathetic beings suffering eternal damnation in Bosch's 'The Garden of Earthly Delights'.

The film was photographed once again by Ronnie Taylor, who had previously worked with Argento on *Opera*. His work here is of a more sumptuous nature, perfectly capturing the elegance and the squalor of the period.

The 'Caligula-esque' bathhouse is also visually striking, featuring a hotbed of sexual and moral depravity. The orgy of unappealing naked flesh on display and the violent outburst related to a debate about the work of Baudelaire, whose writing on sex and death seem perfectly at home in the work of Argento, all play out under the steam and heat generated by the saunas and the copulating masses. It's a credit to

Argento and production designer Antonello Geleng (who also worked with Argento on *The Stendhal Syndrome*) that, in scenes like this, one can almost smell the sweat oozing from every frame.

The shots inside the auditorium are rhapsodic, as Argento's camera appears to float around, showing off the décor and exquisite detail. Patrons of opera houses in these times simply attended to show off their status within society and very little attention was languished on the actual opera. Audience members were more concerned with socialising, flirting or being fitted for extravagant new clothes, and this is all present in Argento's film, perhaps his most meticulously researched and planned project. A staggering 900 extras were also employed for these scenes.

Argento regular Sergio Stivaletti once again provided special effects, including the huge rat trap containing deformed humans that appears in a dream sequence, and a small army of animatronic rodents. As well as all the blood and gore the film is drenched in, Stivaletti also created the Parisian skyline for the scenes set on the roof of the opera house.

Phantom of the Opera was actually Argento's third period film (the other two being *The Five Days of Milan* and *The Wax Mask*, which he produced). The costumes, designed by Agnes Gyarmathy, are as lavish and splendid as the set design. Despite the period setting, the film has a distinct postmodern slant. The Phantom resembles a moody rock star, complete with leather trousers, flowing locks and pouty posturing.

Themes

In his more recent films such as *Jenifer*, *Pelts* and *Mother of Tears*, Argento has been exploring a rather seedy arena of abhorrent sexuality that he initially touched upon in *Phantom of the Opera*, generating subversive horror from sexuality, coitus and the human body. In a scene reminiscent of the beginning of *Batman Returns* (1992), the Phantom, abandoned at birth by his parents, is set adrift down a river and retrieved from the water by rats that go on to raise him as one of their own. His animalistic tendencies are not only evident in his violent acts towards anyone unfortunate enough to cross his path, but also in his dubious relationship with his rodent family. After he makes love with Christine, the Phantom also seeks sexual gratification from the rats that share his home, allowing them to crawl over his genitals. Argento had touched upon incestuous relationships before – in *Cat O'Nine Tails* and *Four Flies on Grey Velvet*, with Professor Terzi and his daughter Anna, and Nina and Roberto respectively.

Argento briefly touches on the claustrophobic and stifling atmosphere rampant in *Suspiria*, with overbearing authority figures and bullying peers. In the scene where a young girl returns to her ballet class after witnessing the death of a paedophilic patron at the hands of the Phantom, she is severely reprimanded by her teacher for having too vivid an imagination and is taunted by her classmates. This brings to mind Suzy and her predicament in *Suspiria*.

The fairytale-like narration in *Suspiria* and *Phenomena* also occurs briefly at the beginning of this film with a disembodied voice informing us of the mysterious bond forged between the abandoned child and the 'inhabitants of darkness'. The story in many ways resembles a subversion of *Beauty and the Beast*, another tale of unrequited love and deceiving appearances.

Drapes feature heavily in the film, as they draw back to reveal the stage, cover over doorways that lead into darkness and hide away the secrets of the opera house that are bursting to be revealed.

Music

Ennio Morricone provides an evocative orchestral score that, considering some of his other work with Argento, is quite mediocre. Sweeping motifs provide tender melodies and a decadent love theme, whereas moments of suspense are catered for by a haunting, progressively suspenseful touch.

Trivia

Argento's friend George Romero actually visited the set in Hungary during filming. He was also there scouting for locations for his proposed version of *The Raven*, a project he later abandoned.

Verdict

This was a daring move by Argento, but one that was ultimately flawed. The film is patchy and anachronistic; many of the technical aspects, while characteristically dazzling, seem to contradict the elegant period in which the narrative is set. While Argento's ever-experimental spirit is on display, it just can't disguise the fact that this irreverent take on Leroux's sordid tale is thoroughly ridiculous. More 'Carry on Argento' than the dark and sensuous Gothic-fantasy it could have been.

THE NEO-ANIMAL TRILOGY

Sleepless was hailed by critics as the comeback of a director who had never been away. The critical mauling his later work had received, up until *Sleepless*, highlights the fact that Argento has never been able to break away from the reputation of his 'golden era'. No matter how daring or experimental each subsequent film, critics and fans inevitably compare them to *Deep Red*, *Suspiria* and *The Bird with the Crystal Plumage*. Great films these may be, but few take into account the fact that Argento is not a director content to remix past glories for a new audience; he is constantly exploring the dark realms of his subconscious, pushing forward new ideas in exciting and progressive ways.

Nonhosonno/Sleepless (2001)

'God only knows what else is buried in my mind.'

Directed/Written/Produced by: Dario Argento
Co-written by: Franco Ferrini & Carlo Lucarelli
Produced by: Claudio Argento
Music by: Goblin
Cinematography: Ronnie Taylor BSC
Edited by: Anna Rosa Napoli AMC
Production Designer: Antonello Geleng
Special Effects: Sergio Stivaletti
Cast: Max von Sydow (Ulisse Moretti), Stefano Dionisi (Giacomo), Chiara Caselli (Gloria), Roberto Zibetti (Lorenzo), Gabriele Lavia (Dr Betti), Paolo

Maria Scalondro (Inspector Manni), Barbara Lerici (Angela)
Also known as: *I Can't Sleep, Non ho sonno*

Synopsis

Retired Detective Moretti is called in to help the police investigate a series of brutal murders linked by paper animals left at the scene of each crime. He begins to suspect that the legendary Killer Dwarf, accused of a previous spate of murders 17 years ago, has returned to terrorise Turin. He is aided in his investigation by a troubled young man whose mother was believed to have been a victim of the Killer Dwarf. Could the psychopath have returned from the dead, or is this a new killer recreating events from the past for some twisted purpose?

Background

Argento collaborated with regular co-writer Franco Ferrini and renowned *giallo* author Carlo Lucarelli to produce what he regarded as one of his best scripts in years, and the director relished going back to his *giallo* roots.

Sleepless was shot in Turin during the summer of 2000; the director chose to shoot here again because of the city's bewitching atmosphere.

Argento had contemplated making another *giallo* for a while, and had been hounded by fans to either make 'another *Deep Red*' or complete his 'Three Mothers' trilogy. *Sleepless* does indeed recall elements of *Deep Red* and has much in common with his early work such as the 'Animal' trilogy. However, it has a much tighter plot that isn't as prone to meander into overtly abstract territory.

When the film premiered in Turin in early 2001, it was met with extremely positive reviews and critics declared it a 'return to form' for the director. It went on to become Argento's biggest hit for over a decade.

In what appears to be a nod to previous films, Argento once again cast Gabriele Lavia (*Deep Red* and *Inferno*) as one of the film's many red herrings.

Max Von Sydow liked the night-black humour evident in the script and he was familiar with Argento's reputation and keen to collaborate with him. As the actor didn't feel comfortable performing soliloquies, he stipulated that a parrot be added to these scenes to act as a confidant.

Chiara Caselli trained for six weeks to learn how to play the harp believably, and she had previously worked on *Nero* (1992), a film produced by Claudio Argento. She and her co-star Stefano Dionisi had been in a relationship prior to filming.

Comments

Sleepless received the most favourable reviews of the director's recent work. There were, of course, those who lamented the glories of *Suspiria* and *Deep Red* and insisted that Argento's apparent downward trajectory was continuing with *Sleepless*. While each of Argento's films is different from the next, one can still see an organic evolution in his distinct oeuvre.

It is particularly evident when considering the films in this chapter that Argento has attempted to move with the times and introduce elements of contemporary culture and technology into his work. Stylistically these films are different; the plots are tighter, the imagery slicker and the violence, to an extent, has been toned down. With the exception of *The Card Player*, Argento's protagonists still solve crimes in an abstract way, utilising art, literature and concepts to catch the killer.

These films bear the mark of a 'new Argento', one who proves yet again he can move with the times while still remaining unique and true to his roots.

Style/Technical

Ronnie Taylor returns to the Argento fold for a third time and again provides faultless cinematography. *Sleepless* has a distinctly modern, slick look that sits comfortably with the urban setting and the contemporary slant Argento is aiming for; the dark and moody atmosphere is interrupted on a regular basis with splashes of red, usually erupting from savagely penetrated bodies.

Argento claimed that with *Sleepless* he was rediscovering the spirit of the camera. Smooth tracking shots and point-of-view angles are once again abundant and breathtaking.

Argento wanted to convey the childish and frenzied theatrics of the killer's mind, and this is evident in the film's opening set piece, on board an empty night train, hurtling through the dark. Angela is tirelessly pursued through the deserted carriages, followed ceaselessly by the camera, except when it cuts to brief exterior shots of the train, highlighting how vulnerable and isolated she is, and how nightmarish her predicament. The camera charges after her, whipping up an intense and feverish atmosphere. Taylor's subjective photography ensures we have no idea when or where the inevitable point of contact between her and the killer will come from, as her stalker seems to possess the potential to emerge out of the periphery of every frame. Tension is racked up and the bloody payoff is exceptionally cruel.

A rather astounding camera track, along a red carpet backstage at the opera house where Gloria is performing in a concert, recalls similar bravura camerawork in *Tenebrae* and *Opera*. We see a myriad of feet coming and going along the carpet as the camera glides along it: stagehands, audience members returning to their seats, ballerinas flitting off to the stage, cleaners vacuuming the carpet, and the killer stalking Gloria. Eventually the camera prowls off the carpet into a dressing room and, still only revealing events from ground level, we glimpse the twitching legs of a dainty ballerina having the life throttled out of her. Moments later her severed head falls to the floor with a sickening thud and the killer moves on. This is all featured in one take, once again exemplifying Argento's skill and technical expertise.

Themes

Argento revisits a few familiar themes in *Sleepless* and returns with one of his favourite motifs: the Freudian killer, whose unleashed repressed memories result in a spate of bloody murders. With a twist. The killer in *Sleepless*, while still rooted in a past evident in his obsession with a children's poem, is not killing to keep a dark secret safe or to protect a loved one; he kills simply because he is evil and, more disturbingly, has come of age.

Like *Deep Red*, the film opens with a flashback of a young child witnessing the rather graphic death of a parent. Argento toys with the idea that most psychological damage occurs during an individual's early years. Childhood, as in *Deep Red*, is presented as inherently sinister and warped. The director has commented that he believes there is a 'heartlessness' about young children that he finds menacing.

The fact that victims are chosen because of their resemblance to specific animals from the creepy poem, while mildly ridiculous, also fits chillingly with this particular killer and his grotesque immaturity. The themed murders recall those of *Se7en* (1995) and its precursor *The Abominable Dr Phibes* (1971).

The imagery of children's toys that was ever present in *Deep Red* reoccurs here too. Moretti's death, when he is menaced by a child's clockwork puppet, mirrors that of Giordani in *Deep Red*. The puppet is essentially a decoy used to evoke memories of the killer dwarf accused of the previous murders. The murders are all based on a nursery rhyme and childish paper cut-outs of animals are left at the scene of each murder. Even the very title of the film, *Non ho sonno* (Italian for 'I can't sleep'), conjures up connotations of childhood anxiety and the corruption of innocence.

The relationship between Moretti and Giacomo is reminiscent of Franco Arno and Carlo Giordani in *Cat O'Nine Tails*, the older man almost a surrogate father for the younger. The warm rapport when young and old pair up to solve a crime is also evident in *Phenomena* and, like that film, tragedy also strikes in *Sleepless*, resulting in one character having to grow up and continue their journey into darkness alone.

The past returning to haunt the present reoccurs in *Sleepless* and, much as in the 'Animal' trilogy, *Deep Red, Tenebrae, Opera, Trauma* and *Giallo*, the killer cannot let go of the past and aims to relive it through each ensuing kill. In a sly nod to Argento's own work, the dwarf accused of the previous murders, Vincenzo De Fabritiis, is a writer of *giallo* novels. The idea of a creator of such work being responsible for blood-fuelled crimes echoes Peter Neal in *Tenebrae* and Marco in *Opera*.

Argento pays more attention to the details of the police investigation in *Sleepless* than he has in many of his previous films; indeed, one of the protagonists is a retired detective. Moretti struggles to come to terms with technology and modern forensics; he prefers old-fashioned methods of investigation. As this is a *giallo*, the modes of detection are still quite abstract. The reliability (or not) of memory and the recalling of past events in order to identify key evidence is important in *Sleepless*. Giacomo must recall the fateful day his mother was murdered, something he has been desperately trying to forget, in order to pinpoint a strange noise heard at the scene of that crime, one of many clues scattered throughout the film. This seemingly insignificant noise becomes paramount in solving the new outbreak of murders. The ageing Moretti, verging on senile, has difficulty remembering things and, just as it seems he has recalled vital information, he is dispatched in a chilling and strangely melancholic scene. The death of a protagonist halfway through the film reflects the similarly unexpected turn of events in Hitchcock's *Psycho* (1960).

The notion of insomnia caused by the inability to forget macabre events is highlighted when Vincenzo's mother Laura claims she hasn't slept since her son's death 17 years ago. When it is revealed that she killed him to protect him, memories of other tortured matriarchs in Argento's films come bubbling to the surface: Martha in *Deep Red*, Frau Brückner in *Phenomena* and Adriana in *Trauma* all committed murder to protect or avenge their offspring and the dark secrets embracing them. Lorenzo's father Dr Betti (Gabriele Lavia) appears to be a continuation of Carlo from *Deep Red* – he knows who the killer is and would do anything to prevent anyone from finding out. The house of the dwarf, where Moretti and Giacomo encounter Laura, resembles the 'haunted' villa of *Deep Red* and the houses of the Three Mothers, and it contains just as many blood-gorged secrets.

After *Deep Red*, the majority of Argento's protagonists had been strong and resourceful women. In what seems like a throwback to his 'Animal' trilogy, however, the lead in *Sleepless* is once again a young man and, like in *Deep Red*, he is aided by a level-headed and intelligent woman. Unlike previous protagonists, though, Giacomo has a personal interest in solving the murders and he hasn't simply stumbled into proceedings by accident like Sam in *The Bird with the Crystal Plumage*, Arno in *Cat O'Nine Tails* or Marc in *Deep Red*. Giacomo, much like the fragile protagonists of *Trauma*, has a troubled past. He is haunted by the memory of his mother's murder and is a recovering alcoholic.

A children's poem entitled 'The Death Farm' provides a catalyst for the killer's psychosis in *Sleepless*. It details a psychotic farmer's grim revenge on the farm animals that have kept him awake, and the killer replicates the murders described in the poem when dispatching his victims. Like the painting in *The Bird with the Crystal Plumage* and the child's drawing and lullaby in *Deep Red*, art, here in the form of poetry, provides both clues to the killer's identity and the inspiration for the killer himself.

Music

Argento had initially approached Serbian composer Goran Bregovic to compose the score for *Sleepless*; however, after beginning work on the soundtrack, the musician requested more money, which Argento refused to pay. The director then persuaded Goblin to reunite for one last score, and they were happy to do this for the man who had given them their big break scoring *Deep Red*. The result is a pulse-pounding, nerve-shredding experience featuring jagged electric guitar riffs and more tender moments courtesy of a melodic, piano-led melody. Of course, no Goblin score would be complete without the obligatory children's lullaby theme, which here resembles a slowly winding down music-box.

Trivia

The poem used in the film, 'The Death Farm', was written by Asia Argento. The name of the parrot is a reference to Von Sydow's friend Marcello Mastroianni, star of Fellini's *8½* (1963).

Verdict

Argento's *giallo* for the modern age is one of his most conventional and concise scripts to date. Pre-empting the harsh logic of *The Card Player* and discarding the baroque trimmings of glories past, *Sleepless* excises the narrative digressions and ambiguity Argento is famed for. The tightly coiled story is precise and there is an uncharacteristic amount of attention paid to it. That said, the director still astounds with visual flourishes and rhapsodic violence and the story unfolds with rabid enthusiasm.

Il cartaio/The Card Player (2003)

Directed/Written/Produced by: Dario Argento
Co-written by: Franco Ferrini
Executive Produced by: Claudio Argento
Music by: Claudio Simonetti
Cinematography: Benoît Debie
Edited by: Walter Fasano AMC
Art Direction: Antonello Geleng & Marina Pinzuti
Special Effects: Sergio Stivaletti
Cast: Stefania Rocca (Anna Mari), Liam Cunningham (John Brennan), Silvio Muccino (Remo), Adalberto Maria Merli (Questore/Police Commissioner), Antonio Cantafora (Inspector Marini), Fiore Argento (Lucia)
Also known as: *Deathsite*

Synopsis

After receiving an anonymous email inviting her to a game of online poker, Detective Anna Mari discovers that the stakes in this game are particularly high; she is playing for someone's life. Unfolding events reveal that a serial killer known only as 'The Card Player' is kidnapping women and forcing the police to play poker for the lives of his victims.

Background

The Card Player began life as a Venice-based sequel to *The Stendhal Syndrome*, entitled *In the Dark*, and looked set to further follow the experiences of Anna Manni. Asia Argento, however, was unable to get involved in the project as she had just finished *xXx* (2002) and wanted to accept other roles. The character was altered slightly to become Anna Mari, the script was tightened and the location moved from the potentially expensive Venice to comparatively cheap Rome. The daily Roman routine of firing a cannon on the hills above the city was also used as a pivotal plot point.

Working with a lower budget than usual, Argento had $2 million to shoot his latest venture in March 2004.

Comments

The Card Player is perhaps one of Argento's most mainstream films and is akin to many US cop shows such as *NYPD Blue*, *Homicide: Life on the Streets* and the *CSI* series. While critics deemed it 'generic', for an Argento film it is actually quite daring, as it once again demonstrates his defiance of expectations and his exploration of a new approach to the traditional *giallo* formula.

It is essentially a police procedural thriller along the lines of *Se7en* (1995) or *Kiss the Girls* (1997), and we follow the detectives as they try to track down a thrill-seeking serial killer who utilises modern technology as a way to wreak havoc and bloody mayhem.

Technology as a tool for conducting deadly activities is a new theme for Argento. The director is keen to show how police procedures have advanced over the years and how technology is increasingly employed to snare criminals, something he touched on in *Sleepless* and *Four Flies on Grey Velvet*. In taking this approach, he once again proved he was fully capable of moving with the times.

Much like the actors in *Two Evil Eyes*, those involved in *The Card Player* were mainly from a theatrical background and provide perhaps the most credible and sturdy performances of any Argento film. The director admired the rugged charisma of Cunningham and the actor's forthright attitude gained him the part. Argento had wanted to work with Stefania Rocca for some time; she was originally approached to play Sonia/Marta in *The Wax Mask*. Argento was happy to let Rocca and Cunningham improvise much of their dialogue, and the onscreen chemistry between the two is undeniable.

Mathieu Kassovitz was initially approached to play the male lead, but he declined in order to film his directorial debut, *Gothika* (2003).

Style/Technical

With *The Card Player*, Argento displays none of the extravagance usually associated with his work. From the film's cold and sterile look, courtesy of *Irreversible* (2002) cinematographer Benoît Debie, to its teasingly restrained violence, mainly occurring offscreen, Argento has fashioned a *gialloesque* thriller that looks unlike any of his others.

Preferring to induce chills by showing the after effects of the murders, his camera hovers over each cadaver like a just-expelled spirit glancing back at its empty vessel and considering it in grim close-up, before departing to the afterlife. The film's various autopsies are filmed with a clinical precision and almost childlike fascination. Argento even creates a moment to jolt the audience out of their seats in one of these scenes.

A prowling camera follows the characters through their computer-filled offices and the shadowy streets of Rome.

The script is as reliant on set pieces as earlier films, but that's not to say Argento doesn't still manage to surprise with a few jaw-droppers, notably the watery demise of computer whizz-kid Remo. Forced to make a life-altering choice and ultimately dragged to his death by a speedboat on a deserted river, this scene is lit only by the distant city lights and an ominous spotlight onboard the boat.

While the murder set pieces are relatively bloodless, they are as sadistic as you would expect from Argento, with his hapless victims being dispatched by a razorblade, whilst being filmed live on a web cam.

The film is shot with minimal lighting and Debie relied on the use of neon and sodium to create the film's cold, modern look. While many of Rome's famous sights are indeed on display, Argento wanted to view the city through a stranger's eyes. After viewing Debie's work on Gasper Noe's *Irreversible*, Argento was convinced he was perfect for the job. The film is frozen under a sheet of cool blues, bright whites and deepest blacks.

The killer's hideout is surrounded by a strange plant, the pollen of which is seen wafting through the air – reminiscent of the strangely ethereal dream sequences in *The Sect* – and the unusual plants were designed by Danilo Bollettini. The clue they provide echoes Marc's quest through various botanical labs in *Deep Red*.

Themes

Unusually for an Argento film, the protagonists in *The Card Player* are not involved in the arts. As cops, they are rooted in a logical world of level-headed investigation and procedural linearity. They utilise rational deduction and analysis to catch the killer, not the usual 'Argentoesque' methods involving misinterpreted events. These sleuths deal only in scientific facts and hard evidence.

John Brennan is an Irish cop on secondment to the British Embassy in Rome after a botched police raid resulted in the death of a minor. Like many of Argento's protagonists, he is a stranger to the city and an outsider from the beginning. His alcoholism is rooted in his trying to forget dark memories, much like Giacomo in *Sleepless*, Carlo in *Deep Red* and Rod in *Two Evil Eyes*. His relationship with Anna provides the film with a warm heart, reminiscent of *Cat O'Nine Tails* and, to a lesser extent, *Sleepless*.

Anna also has a dark past and was traumatised by the death of her father, a gambling addict who committed suicide. These damaged characters are drawn towards each other and their tentative relationship unfolds during the course of the film. The film's climax harks back to a bygone era of classic thrillers where heroines would be thrust into impending danger; Argento's typically strong and determined heroine, however, manages to free herself and doesn't rely on a man to rescue her.

Technology is presented as a cold and dangerous thing in the film. The sterility of chat-rooms and online games highlights the sinister side of the web, as users often have no idea who they are really chatting to or what they're capable of.

This technological slant is a popular trait in Asian horror films such as *Ringu* (1998), *One Missed Call* (2003) and *Phone* (2002). A number of other films, before and since *The Card Player*, have mined the potential terror that lurks within the Internet – including *feardotcom* (2002), *Hard Candy* (2005), *Untraceable* (2008) and *My Little Eye* (2002) – to varying degrees of success/crassness.

With one of the main themes of the film, addiction, Argento subtly references one of his favourite directors, Fritz Lang, and in particular that director's film *Dr Mabuse the Gambler* (1922) and its portrayal of amoral and desperate actions to gain the attention of an unrequited love. Argento slyly references his own work too; one of the characters is called Professor Terzi, which is a reference to *Cat O'Nine Tails*.

The killer, and indeed the police and several of the victims, are all presented as people who have to deal with risk on a daily basis. One victim is filmed walking in front of a tram, narrowly avoiding being hit by it, and simply wandering on her way. The killer does not suffer from a prior trauma, nor are there any Freudian undertones;

he is simply presented as an insane thrill seeker, intent on getting the attention of Anna.

The poker games played throughout the film seem to be doubling as a metaphor for living life; characters discuss strategies and the differing methods of players, and these could easily lend themselves to descriptions of how different people live their lives. It's a tenuous link, but one that Argento broaches with sincerity. Then again, that could just be his poker face.

Argento slyly subverts his usual use of art as a means of causing harm in one scene: Anna is alerted to the presence of the killer in her home when she catches his reflection in a spherical glass ornament. She holds a magnifying glass to the ornament to enlarge the reflection and try to identify the intruder. This use of ornamental art as a tool to locate the killer is a vintage Argento moment – obscure, bizarre and beautifully absurd.

Another element that could be described as vintage Argento comes in the shape of the tap-dancing, opera-singing morgue attendant who recalls the oddball characters that peppered Argento's earlier films.

Music

Claudio Simonetti provides a techno-infused bombastic score that accentuates the film's nerve-shredding and hysterical pace. It's a high-octane and frantically pounding soundtrack that would easily fill dance floors favouring Kraut techno. Glitches, bleeps and thudding beats herald Argento's embrace of twenty-first-century technology.

Trivia

Vera Gemma, who plays the third victim of the killer, also starred in her friend Asia's directorial debut *Scarlet Diva*. Gemma's father, actor Giuliano Gemma, played Inspector Germani in *Tenebrae*.

Verdict

Following on from *Sleepless*, Argento attempts to further embed himself in the twenty-first century with *The Card Player*. Cutting and pasting typical *giallo* elements into a conventional psycho-thriller flick, the film exhibits little of the director's usual flair or creativity and is at times as anonymous as a timid online chat-room user. The ending, though, while bittersweet, is surely one of Argento's most optimistic and the film is solidly entertaining with two of Argento's most engrossing leads.

Ti piace Hitchcock? /Do You Like Hitchcock? (2005)

Directed/Written by: Dario Argento
Co-written by: Franco Ferrini
Produced by: Claudio Argento
Music by: Pino Donaggio
Cinematography: Frederic Fasano
Edited by: Walter Fasano AMC
Special Effects: Sergio Stivaletti
Cast: Elio Germano (Giulio), Chiara Conti (Federica), Elisabetta Rocchetti (Sasha), Iván Morales (Andrea), Cristina Brondo (Arianna), Elena Maria Bellini (Giulio's Mother)

Synopsis

Film student Giulio enjoys watching the residents of the building across the street from his flat. When a woman is brutally murdered, he suspects foul play on the part of her daughter. He believes she and another woman have been inspired to kill off people in each other's lives, just like the plot of Hitchcock's *Strangers on a Train*. Putting his own life at risk and utilising his knowledge of classic Hitchcock, Giulio sets out to find the killer.

Background

Do You Like Hitchcock? was the first in a proposed series of made-for-TV films commissioned by RAI Trade, an Italian international sales company. They also co-produced the film and distributed it. Argento was invited to take part in the project and saw it as the perfect opportunity to pay homage to Hitchcock. With a mere $4 million, filming took place in July 2004 in Argento's old stomping ground, Turin.

Comments

Argento has spent much of his career being compared with Hitchcock. Both are purveyors of tense, violent and subversive films that remain as shocking today as they did upon initial release. Both are technical masters who revel in experimenting with new and exciting ways to tell a story. However, Hitchcock was a very linear director – he stuck rigidly to storyboards and told stories in a logical manner, culminating in the carefully prepared climax. Argento is the opposite; his style and flamboyance are utilised to tell stories, the details of which come second to how they are conveyed through images and visual extravagance.

They also share a love of Freud, psychoanalysis, the mechanics of suspense and fear, the ordinary everyman thrust into wild and tempestuous situations, and often damaging familial relationships, particularly those between mothers and their children.

While Argento deliberately references the work of Hitchcock during the course of the film, the work of the Master is also integral to the plot of the Maestro's latest venture.

It is easy to see why Argento has been compared to Hitchcock, and, much as he may have resented it initially, this film really shows that there is substance to his reputation as a 'garlic-flavoured Hitchcock'. This is, above all else, a very playful film. It is essentially Argento having fun and allowing his inner film geek to come out to play. *Do You Like Hitchcock?* is a love letter to Alfred Hitchcock and fans of cinema alike. Much fun can be garnered from spotting references to other cinematic classics too.

The film is full of deliberate references, from the film posters that adorn the walls of the video shop and Giulio's flat – including *Vertigo*

(1958), *Psycho* (1960), *Dial M for Murder* (1954) and Argento's own *The Card Player* – to the films Giulio watches. These include *Metropolis* (1927), *The Golem* (1920) – a film Argento previously considered remaking – *Nosferatu* (1922) and *Man with a Movie Camera* (1929). Various shots mirroring those in some of Hitchcock's films, such as *Rear Window* (1954), *Vertigo* and *Psycho*, to name but a few, are also evident. Argento even references his own *The Bird with the Crystal Plumage* in the scene where Sasha's mother is killed in front of her window, her death as much on display as Monica's struggle with her attacker was.

Argento's own back catalogue is mined for fun as much as Hitchcock's; note the bath scene that echoes events in *Deep Red*, *Two Evil Eyes* and Mario Bava's *Blood and Black Lace* (1964). Andrea's automobile-related death is a pared-down version of Carlo's in *Deep Red*.

These references don't take on the smug postmodern and deconstructive nature of those in the likes of Kevin Williamson scripts; they are loving tributes and mostly necessary to furthering the story. For those who don't get every reference, it will not detract from their enjoyment of the film. Although this is a TV film and very tame compared with his other films, Argento does still manage to push the boundaries in terms of sex and violence and it still offers unsuspecting audiences a few jolts here and there.

Style/Technical

Frederic Fasano, who was also the cinematographer on *Scarlet Diva*, photographs events in a clean and precise manner. There are no flamboyant or indulgent flourishes on show, which is a shame really.

The realist look of the film is very conventional and typical of Argento's slick approach as evident in *Sleepless*, *The Card Player* and *Giallo*. The tone is consistently light and playful and the young, sexy cast, who for some reason have been dubbed with awful 'mockney' accents, all seem to be having fun.

Many of the scenes unfold as pastiches of the conventions of suspense, and it would appear that the film has been edited carefully and, dare I say it, conventionally. Gone are the disorientating cuts from extreme close-ups to wider shots and back again. As much as the film flows, it certainly lacks the usual flavour of an Argento movie. This is perhaps the most linear of Argento's plots. Following on from *The Card Player*, *Do You Like Hitchcock?* pays just as much close attention to the story and is perhaps one of the director's most accessible films.

The city of Turin becomes a character in its own right, with the many shots of imposing buildings and baroque architecture. Its lay-out and design are inherent to the plot as they enable Giulio to gaze across the street into the lives of his neighbours.

Themes

The film is essentially a compilation of scenes where characters watch each other and analyse why they do it and what they see. Voyeurism, perception and spying are all on display throughout the film. Giulio as a young boy spies on two women in the forest; as a young man he watches his neighbours go about their daily routines à la *Rear Window*; he spies on the liaisons between Federica and her boss; the neighbours watch each other and the rubber-necking crowd gather around Andrea's body in the middle of the road, not to help, just to watch.

The audience are constantly reminded of their role as spectators too. We see everything that Giulio sees and he often puts his own life at risk in order to see things he really shouldn't see.

Giulio and his girlfriend Arianna are both university students. Of the two, she is presented as the more rational and logical, constantly dismissing Giulio's theories as madcap and unrealistic. She tells him that his head has been warped by watching so many movies and he is losing his grip on reality as a result. However, when Giulio breaks his leg and is rendered immobile (guess which Hitchcock film?), Arianna throws herself head first into the investigation and gets so caught up in the excitement and danger that she, as with Giulio before her, puts herself in mortal danger, seemingly for the sake of a thrill.

Despite Arianna's allegations that he has an overactive imagination, Giulio is proved right about Sasha and the murder and proves that he can differentiate between film and reality. Is this another dig from Argento at critics who blame horror films and onscreen violence for social unrest and violence outside the multiplex? It would appear Argento's take on this is quite clear.

Giulio is a typical example of Argento's, and indeed Hitchcock's, everyman protagonist thrust into a perilous situation. His actions throughout the film submerge him further in the mystery. Like many of Argento's protagonists, he takes it upon himself to investigate the mysterious occurrences. His natural curiosity, initially presented to us in the scenes where he spies on the women in the forest as a young boy, will no doubt be his downfall; as the closing scene suggests, his nosiness may continue to lead him into dangerous situations. Interestingly, the sexy new occupant of Sasha's flat he spies on with his binoculars is reading a copy of a *giallo* book entitled *A Light in the Window* by Mary Roberts Rinehart.

Hitchcock was very fond of 'doubles' and they are also present in Argento's film in the form of the blonde and mysterious Federica, and the conniving brunette Sasha.

Music

Once again Argento enlisted Brian De Palma regular Pino Donaggio to score. Donaggio's soundtracks for *Two Evil Eyes* and *Trauma* were quite uneven, but he really delivers here. It is a taut, suspenseful score full of frenzied strings and sweeping orchestrations that successfully enhance the unfolding drama as much as pay tribute to Bernard Herrmann's work for Hitchcock.

Verdict

A light, fun and entertaining film from Argento and his first significant
foray into TV for over 25 years. Unfortunately, it doesn't contain any
of the typical flourishes and sparks of brilliance associated with his
usual stylish direction and the events here unfold all too predictably.
Still, it does demonstrate Argento's talent for telling a solid story,
and engaging in some fun with his audience.

For those keen to see exactly what Argento could do with a completely free rein in the usually quite restrictive environment of television, Mick Garris would help provide this opportunity when he
invited Argento to contribute to the *Masters of Horror* series.

BLOOD, SEX & TEARS

'Who wants to eat the girl?'

Jenifer (2005)

Directed by: Dario Argento
Screenplay by: Steven Weber
Based on a short story by: Bruce Jones
Music by: Claudio Simonetti
Cinematography: Attila Szalay
Edited by: Marshall Harvey
Production Designer: David Fischer
Cast: Steven Weber (Frank Spivey), Carrie Anne Fleming (Jenifer), Brenda James (Ruby), Harris Allan (Pete), Beau Starr (Chief Charlie), Julia Arkos (Ann Wilkerson), Cynthia Garris (Rose)

Synopsis

Detective Frank Spivey rescues a young woman from being murdered by a crazed man. Appalled by the woman's deformity, he takes pity on her and takes her in. Her presence, however, has horrific effects on the rest of his family and soon Frank is plunged into a nightmare of obsession, addiction and lust, as Jenifer becomes the centre of his world.

Background

Mick Garris created *Masters of Horror* to showcase the work of relatively new genre directors alongside those who inspired them

– revealing the latter to be just as raw and relevant now as in their heydays. Each filmmaker was promised free rein and no limitations – the whole point was to go as over-the-top in terms of screen violence and horror as they desired. Argento was keen to get involved when he heard who else was taking part in the project: John Carpenter, Tobe Hooper, Joe Dante and John Landis, to name a few. These were directors whom Argento had wanted to be identified with when he made the likes of *Two Evil Eyes* and *Trauma*. He got his wish, though his legions of fans would argue he is still in a league of his own!

Jenifer itself is based on a story from the comic *Creepy* and adapted for the screen by Steven Weber, who also stars. Argento made a few changes to the script to tailor it to his own taste. Initial preparation for *Jenifer* was carried out largely by email between Argento and the show's creators. He was still in Rome putting the finishing touches to *Do You Like Hitchcock?* Not really accustomed to making films this way, Argento apparently enjoyed the process and claimed it left no room for unpleasant surprises. Details of actors and locations were emailed back and forth until the director was satisfied he was able to make the film he wanted to make.

Despite the language barrier, Argento was still able to convey what he wanted for the film, much as he did on *Two Evil Eyes* and *Trauma*. He and Steven Weber even forged a close friendship during filming, going as far as discussing whether they would fall for someone like Jenifer in real life. Their conclusion? Yes, apparently they would!

Comments

Argento was one of only two directors in the series to actually take full advantage of the creative freedom the project offered, Takashi Miike being the other – and his episode was never broadcast as it was deemed so explicit. As a result, Argento's was the only episode with cuts imposed, the producers feeling that some of the imagery was simply too extreme. Two shots depicting Jenifer performing oral sex were removed.

Argento claimed that he wanted to make a 'beautiful' movie and was attracted to the story because of its powerful and disturbing sexuality. Essentially a subversion of *Beauty and the Beast*, *Jenifer* marks the beginning of a new phase in Argento's career. This film and those which followed, *Pelts*, *Mother of Tears* and *Giallo* demonstrate the director's preoccupation with abhorrent sexuality and carnality. Argento has seemingly discovered a whole new way to shock and provoke people, and he lenses it so elegantly that it is just as disturbing as the violence still evident in his work of this new era.

Style/Technical

Cinematographer Attila Szalay was one of three directors of photography on the series. He and Argento wanted to create a comic-book feel, faithful to the origins of the script. The heavily stylised and atmospheric lighting reveals enough of the horrific images of cannibalistic sexuality to pack a real punch.

A few trademark Argento flashes occur in *Jenifer*, namely in the violent attacks and deranged sexuality. When Argento approached Carrie Anne Fleming to play the titular character, the actress grasped the opportunity, completely losing herself in the part and shedding all inhibitions. She was aided by terrific make-up effects, courtesy of the KNB EFX group, rendering her completely unrecognisable.

Digital effects were wisely kept to a minimum. Greg Nicotero was responsible for enhancing Jenifer's ghoulish appearance after her make-up had been applied. In post-production he digitally enlarged her eyes to shocking effect. When we do see her whole face, it is chilling to the core.

At first, Argento offers us only glimpses of the horror lurking beneath her blonde waves; a curled lip here, a soulless and dark eye there.

Although Argento has often 'sexualised' violence in his films, capturing it stylishly and unflinchingly, *Jenifer* seems to be the logical culmination of the ideas of violence and sexuality he has incorporated into his work. Steven Weber described *Jenifer* as 'gritty, bloody, horror porn' – a term that could arguably be applied to much of Argento's output. In saying that, his work is still more considered and opulent than the current spate of 'horror-porn' films such as the *Saw* (2004) and *Hostel* (2005) series.

Themes

Duality in characters has always been an interest of Argento's. In films such as *Deep Red*, *Phenomena* and *Trauma*, the duality of mother/ murderer is inherent, and it resurfaces in *Giallo* with Enzo and Yellow. Like those disturbed characters, Jenifer is at times also presented in a sympathetic light – she is to be pitied as much as feared.

In *Jenifer*, Argento aims for the more visceral angle, presenting Jenifer to us as a beauty/beast hybrid. While her face is a distorted and demonic snarl, her body is voluptuous and desirable. She oozes a strange and savage sexuality that seemingly enraptures the males in her vicinity. As awful as some of the acts she commits are, there is also something oddly childlike and naïve about her – she whimpers and sobs in the corner of Frank's bedroom, and when she slaughters his cat she offers it to him as a gift, a token of her love for him, further highlighting her monstrous/childlike personality.

An interesting parallel is drawn between her and Frankenstein's Monster in a darkly amusing parody of the infamous scene in *Frankenstein* (1931) where the Monster regards a little girl with dangerous curiosity.

Throughout the course of the film, various characters comment on Jenifer's morbid duality. An orderly at the hospital where Jenifer is interned comments, 'How'd you get *that* head on *that* body?'

Unlike many of Argento's characters, Jenifer seems to exist almost without a past. No one knows where she came from or who she is. Argento described her as being an alien, but Fleming and Weber saw her more as a feral outcast, instinctual and raw and wholly incapable of living within civilised society. Her ambiguity adds to the horror and pity she generates.

The abhorrent sexuality Argento has been exploring in his recent work is fully evident in *Jenifer*. As mentioned, there were a couple of shots cut from the final film that depicted Jenifer performing oral sex on Frank and biting Rose's son's penis off. Argento was interested in the idea of a woman with a monstrous mouth performing pleasurable acts on a man. This notion has distinct connotations of the 'vagina dentata' – a concept explored more thoroughly, yet for morbid laughs, in *Teeth* (2008) – and is linked to the idea of women as castrators, disempowering men. The shot involving Rose's son is another example of the violence inflicted on children in Argento's work. The young girls of *Phenomena*, the toddlers in *Mother of Tears*, and, of course, the little girl who meets a ghastly end when confronted by Jenifer in her backyard, prove no one is safe in an Argento movie – not even the young.

Verdict

Argento claims that *Jenifer* is unique in his body of work as it is his only love story. In what is basically a made-for-TV movie, *Jenifer* really pushes boundaries in terms of what is acceptable primetime viewing. Not merely an interesting footnote in Argento's oeuvre, but a fully realised and haunting fairytale that will linger in the mind long after viewing. *Jenifer* is one of the nastiest and most memorable instalments of the whole *Masters of Horror* series.

Pelts (2006)

Directed by: Dario Argento
Screenplay by: Matt Venne
Based on a short story by: F Paul Wilson

Music by: Claudio Simonetti
Cinematographer: Attila Szalay
Edited by: Marshall Harvey
Production Designer: David Fischer
Cast: Meat Loaf Aday (Jake Feldman), Ellen Ewusie (Shana), John Saxon (Jeb Jameson), Brenda McDonald (Mother Mayter), Link Baker (Lou Chinaski), Elise Lew (Sue Chin Yao), Michal Suchánek (Larry Jameson)

Synopsis

Luckless furrier Jake acquires a strange collection of racoon pelts from Jeb Jameson. He plans to fashion them into a coat and present it to Shana, an exotic dancer he is in love with. However, all who come into contact with the mystical furs meet horrible demises, all of which are self-inflicted. When Jake finally presents the finished coat to Shana, he has a few other things he'd like to offer her, including his own skin.

Background

Based on a short story by F Paul Wilson and adapted for the screen by Matt Venne, *Pelts* is a gleefully sadistic little tale of greed, lust and dangerous desire. Argento was attracted to the strange story of people driven to insanity and self-mutilation by their obsessions and vanity.

Comments

Argento's second offering to the *Masters of Horror* series was described by its creator Mick Garris as the season's 'wet episode'. Argento enthusiastically drenches almost every scene in blood and sinew.

When Argento approached Meat Loaf to play the role of Jake, the actor took the part on his daughter's insistence, as she was a huge fan of the director.

Strangely for an Argento film, there seems to be a definite political undertone examining animal-rights issues. The atrocities inflicted on the racoons are revisited on the humans involved in each stage of the transformation of the hides into a coat, playfully linking vanity and fashion with pain and death.

Pelts also marked the reunion of Argento and his *Tenebrae* star John Saxon, a stalwart of the genre.

Style/Technical

As with *Jenifer*, Argento also creates a distinct comic-book feel with *Pelts*, from the comic font of the titles to the set design and limited colour scheme. The lurid lighting of the strip club and Shana's apartment recall the candy colours of *Suspiria* and *Inferno*.

The ruins where Jeb and Larry find the racoons were lit from the sides to create a magical and mysterious atmosphere quite akin to that conjured in *Phenomena*. Created by production designer David Fischer, they exemplify the film's lyrical visual flair.

Another startling set piece is the fur factory where the hides are treated and transformed into a coat. Filming took place inside a real fur factory and the creepy atmosphere seeps off the screen. Argento also throws in a cheeky reference to his *giallo* films in the scene where the furrier dons black leather gloves and wields a glinting knife to skin the racoons.

Argento laces the tale with imagery of cages and snares, not only those that trap the racoons, but also the ones suggested by the way he frames the characters in certain scenes, highlighting their self-inflicted entrapment as a result of their desire to obtain the unobtainable. This is most notable in the scene with Shana and Jake in the elevator during the film's climax and in that of the seamstress who sews shut her own eyes (a cruel reversal of Betty's torture in *Opera*), nose and mouth, suffocating to death.

In what also appears to be a reference to *Opera*, Jeb and Larry are reflected in the eyes of a racoon, much in the same way that various characters were reflected in the eyes of the ravens in *Opera*, conjuring notions of voyeurism and forbidden glances.

The special effects are a mixture of prosthetics and make-up with digital enhancement, provided again by the KNB EFX group, and are incredibly visceral and effective.

Themes

The body modification throughout *Pelts* recalls similar imagery in *Hellraiser* (1987) and is just as wet and gory.

Argento really nails the combination of erotic and gruesome, exciting and repulsive, much as he did in *Jenifer*. Disturbing images are offered up in feverish and stylish ways. This is especially evident in the various methods by which each of the characters kills themselves.

As soon as they see the racoon furs, they are overcome by their mystical qualities. They seem to provide something that everyone wants for themselves. The furs demonstrate the greed of those who covet them and expose the dark, twisted side of human nature that makes people do despicable things.

The fact that Shana is actually a lesbian and only sleeps with Jake to obtain the furs highlights how much she goes against her own instincts and principles to get what she wants. These characters are literally blinded by their obsessions.

The characters are all driven by greed, each having a downbeat past that they are desperately trying to escape. Jake has been struggling to keep his business afloat and craves the attention of exotic dancer Shana. Shana, a failed model who has turned to stripping to make ends meet, only wants him for his money and a way out of her situation.

A further parallel between the characters and the animals is drawn in the comparison of a racoon so desperate to escape its trap that it chews its own paw off and Shana's similar demise, brought about by her desperation to escape Jake's groping and bloody clutches in the elevator. Her death also mirrors that of Jane in *Tenebrae*, her arm lopped off in a geyser of gore. In an earlier scene, she fends off Jake's sleazy advances by wielding a chair at him, much like a lion tamer, highlighting Jake's animalistic qualities. The characters are all essentially 'hunting' for what they want, but as soon as they obtain it, like a wild animal, it turns on them.

At one stage in the film Jake comments that 'cutting is an art', anticipating his demise by his own hand later on as he slices the skin from his own torso and presents it to Shana, declaring, 'I made this for you, it's my work of art.' Argento once again blurs the line between art and pain.

The strange character of Mater Mayter recalls the Three Mothers and conjures up many fairytale horrors – a creepy old woman living alone in a house in the forest. She explains to Jake that the racoons are sentient beings. She seems like a vaguely supernatural character, knowing full well that Jake was coming to see her and explaining the mythology surrounding her land and the racoons. She is a recluse and a sort of guardian of the forest, walling up her property, not to keep people out, but to keep the strange creatures in. In a very creepy shot, the racoons are seen peering in through the window of the house at Jake and Mater Mayter.

Verdict

While the imagery in *Pelts* is as grotesque as what you might expect from Argento, the film itself is fairly standard. Outside of the 'Three Mothers' trilogy and *Phenomena*, this is the closest Argento has come to filming a fantasy horror. While extremely sadistic, none of his usual flair is evident here, in what is essentially a mildly entertaining and nastily grim little tale.

La Terza madre/Mother of Tears: The Third Mother (2007)

Directed/Written/Produced by: Dario Argento
Co-written by: Jace Anderson & Adam Gierasch
Produced by: Claudio Argento
Music by: Claudio Simonetti

Cinematographer: Frederic Fasano
Edited by: Walter Fasano
Production Designers: Francesca Bocca & Valentina Ferroni
Special Effects: Sergio Stivaletti
Cast: Asia Argento (Sarah Mandy), Cristian Solimeno (Detective Marchi), Adam Jones (Michael Pierce), Moran Atias (Mater Lachrymarum), Daria Nicolodi (Elisa Mandy), Udo Kier (Padre Johannes), Valeria Cavalli (Marta), Coralina Cataldi-Tassoni (Giselle)

Synopsis

After opening a recently exhumed urn from a cemetery outside Rome, young art restoration student Sarah Mandy witnesses her colleague being torn to shreds by three mysterious figures. She soon realises that, by opening the urn, they have unwittingly precipitated the return of a powerful witch known as the Mother of Tears. When Rome is plunged into a new age of darkness, Sarah must master her own latent powers to stop the witch and her hordes of followers from destroying the city and unleashing evil throughout the world.

Background

After 27 years, Argento finally returned to the Three Mothers to complete his trilogy. Initially resenting the pressure to finish the trilogy, the director waited until it felt right to return. Very few filmic instalments have been so long in the making or indeed so anticipated. With a budget of $3.5 million, filming began in October 2006 in various locations throughout Italy, including Turin and Rome.

Due to the artistic freedom Argento was granted with *Jenifer* and *Pelts*, he really let his imagination go to places even he hadn't dared let it go before, dreaming up perhaps some of his cruellest, most sadistic imagery yet. And for Argento that's saying something! Ideas for *Mother of Tears* 'suddenly bubbled over like sparkling champagne', Argento remarked, and the film heralds his entrance into a new arena of sexually sadistic imagery.

Argento teamed up with writers Jace Anderson and Adam Gierasch (who regularly write for Tobe Hooper) after he met them while filming his *Masters of Horror* instalments in the States. He and Claudio Argento believed the time might be right to return to the trilogy after it was announced there would be a remake of *Suspiria*, sparking a resurgence of interest in Argento and a re-evaluation of his previous work.

After viewing the first cut of the film, however, the distribution company Medusa were utterly shocked at its violence and perverse sexuality. They were especially perturbed by the depictions of graphic violence towards children and believed the film wasn't commercial enough. What were they expecting!?

Comments

The Mother of Tears is glimpsed briefly in *Inferno*. She appears to Mark in his lecture theatre while stroking a large white cat, an image that drips all manner of sexual connotations. She also appears in the back of a taxi driving past the scene of Sara and Carlo's deaths. It was suggested in *Inferno* that she dwelt in the Biblioteca where Sara searches for the book by Varelli. However, due to her new dwelling place in *Mother of Tears*, Argento offered that she may have relocated after the deaths of Mater Suspiriorum and Mater Tenebrarum, descending into the catacombs, surrounding herself with the dead and the past. The actress who portrayed her in Inferno was Ania Pieroni, also the sexy shoplifter in *Tenebrae*. Her death in *Tenebrae* was interpreted by critics as Argento's way of killing off any chance of completing the 'Three Mothers' trilogy. Argento admitted he felt pressurised and wasn't prepared to undergo another tortuous relationship with a studio again after the debacle with Fox over *Inferno*. When he did begin the process of drafting a script, he claimed that the film would combine autobiography with 'fantasy and sadness. It will revolve around mysticism, alchemy, terrorism and Gnosticism'. Argento reputedly gave himself nightmares due to all his research into witchcraft.

The film marks a reunion of sorts with several key people who have been significant to Argento throughout his career, notably his daughter Asia Argento and his former partner, Daria Nicolodi. The latter hadn't worked with Argento since he elaborately disposed of her character in *Opera* in 1987. Also joining the cast were Coralina Cataldi-Tassoni (*Demons 2*, *Opera* and *Phantom of the Opera*), Udo Kier (*Suspiria*), a stalwart of the horror genre, and Valeria Cavalli, who had starred in Lamberto Bava's *giallo* film, *A Blade in the Dark* (1983).

Style/Technical

Argento commented that he wanted *Mother of Tears* to be as different from *Suspiria* and *Inferno* as those films were from each other.

Mother of Tears certainly has more of an epic feel to it. Whereas the two prior instalments took place within the confines of one location, this film unfolds as Sarah seeks help throughout Italy in her quest to destroy the Third Mother, in a journey that closely resembles that of Dean Corso in *The Ninth Gate* (1999). Argento makes good use of many locations throughout Rome, presenting us with a modern and bustling cosmopolitan city, but a city still deeply connected with its past by its distinct architecture. It is a perfect setting for a story in which the past comes back to torment the present. The film is set firmly in contemporary society, but when Sarah disposes of her mobile phone, she has to resort to somewhat 'old-fashioned' methods of communication like public phone boxes, highlighting the breakdown of communication within a logical society immersed in an age of technology. Indeed, with cutting-edge technology the world is rendered a much smaller place, making the almost viral epidemic of darkness heralded by Mater Lachrymarum spread far and wide.

The film has a driving narrative momentum that is very unlike the dreamlike and wandering storylines of *Suspiria* and *Inferno*. Sarah is in permanent transience, physically and mentally, as she discovers her own latent powers inherited from her mother, who was a powerful white witch.

This film lacks the glowing and lurid kaleidoscopic look of *Suspiria* and *Inferno*, and it resembles Argento's more recent output, favouring a stylish neo-realism as opposed to baroque surrealism. While much of *Suspiria* and *Inferno* were studio-bound, *Mother of Tears* takes us out into the open countryside and through the winding streets of Rome.

Argento and his director of photography Frederic Fasano, who also acted as cinematographer on *Do You Like Hitchcock?*, *Scarlet Diva* and *Giallo*, wanted to begin the film with cooler, muted tones, gradually melting into red as events become more delirious and violent, before we plunge headfirst into the soaking climax.

Throughout the film we are offered only tantalising glimpses of the Third Mother; a piercing eye here, a pouting lip there, until her, quite literally, full unveiling.

As Sara wanders around the house of Mater Lachrymarum, Argento films her tentative steps in one long, languid shot that easily recalls the brilliance of similar shots in *Tenebrae*, *Opera* and *Sleepless*. The haunting moonlight floating in through the ornate Gothic windows lights her way like a nightmarish rainbow, stirring up memories of the eerie, candy-coloured night walks of *Suspiria* and *Inferno*.

The violence in the film is as savage and overtly theatrical as anything Argento has done before. In several scenes, he really outdoes himself. The opening death of Giselle, as she is torn to pieces and strangled with her own intestines after opening an ancient urn, arguably rivals the opening deaths in *Suspiria* for shear spectacle, intensity and breathtaking brutality.

Mother of Tears also marks the first time that Argento has utilised CGI to such a large extent. The quality of the special effects varies throughout the film (in large part due to the film's limited budget), but the stronger effects remain those created by Sergio Stivaletti.

While he initially envisioned the film as a big-budget epic, Argento unfortunately did not obtain the funding he wanted. (Just imagine how incredible the fall of Rome as envisioned by Argento would have looked had he been given a bigger budget to fully realise his dark dreams.) As it is, he simply presents us with random and isolated pockets of civil unrest and limited bursts of violence. When the city is shown in wider shots, CG raging infernos and reliance on sound effects are all we have to fathom the extent of the anarchy the city is descending into.

Argento also deploys comic-book style strips to convey the flashback sequence detailing the quest of de la Valle (the inhabitant of the exhumed coffin that also contains the urn) as he tried to transfer the urn to the Pope in medieval times.

Of course, no Three Mothers film would be quite complete without a disquieting and hallucinogenic taxi ride. Whilst not as angst-ridden as Suzy's ride into darkness in *Suspiria* or as ear-splittingly unhinged as Sara's in *Inferno*, when Sarah takes a taxi to the house of Mater Lachrymarum, it is a hypnotic and sinister one, with eerily throbbing music and slow, disorientating cuts as Sarah winds her way into the dark heart of Rome. The fact that public transport is still running while Rome self-destructs is a testament to Argento's emphasis on stylistic flair over logical narrative. To point out such discrepancies in a film like *Mother of Tears* is ridiculous, however. It is the distinct lack of logic that lends the film its nightmarish atmosphere and phantasmagorical elements.

Another criticism levelled at the film was the appearance of the congregating witches in Rome. Supposed to represent the ultimate embodiments of evil, they more closely resemble heavily made-up Goths from the eighties on a rowdy girl's night out.

Argento apparently shot much of the film without extensive storyboards, preferring to improvise and experiment. The film yet again demonstrates Argento's unceasing experimentation and his willingness to push himself to extremes.

Mother of Tears is an apocalyptic horror film akin to *The Sect* (1991) or *The Omen* (1976). Its straightforward narrative moves at breakneck pace. Fans of Argento will find much to salivate over here, with gruesome deaths and splashy effects all held together by an almost tongue-in-cheek vibe.

Themes

Some of the imagery in *Mother of Tears* conjures up previous Argento work, notably *Phenomena* and *Jenifer*. The demonic monkey that pursues Sarah through the museum recalls the chimp in *Phenomena*, and Sarah's wading through a pool of decaying bodies towards the film's climax easily recalls Jennifer's struggles in the basement of Frau Brückner's house, also in *Phenomena*.

Violence towards children is another startling theme that reoccurs several times during the film. Heralding the return of Mater Lachrymarum is an outbreak of suicides and murders throughout Rome, commencing with a young mother hurling her toddler off a bridge into the river below.

Argento's interest in eye violation returns with a vengeance in this film. In a scene evoking memories of *A Clockwork Orange* (1971) and *Opera*, Asia Argento has her eye forcibly held open while the Alchemist uses a device that can enable him to see everything she has seen. This pseudo-scientific apparatus with blatant mystical overtones recalls the device used to record the last thing seen by the eyes of the recently deceased in *Four Flies on Grey Velvet*. The Alchemist is also wheelchair-bound, much like Varelli in *Inferno*, a sign in many ways of the decline of alchemy in a modern age.

The demise of Marta's lover occurs when her eyes are snatched out – recalling the eye violation in *Opera* and *Pelts* – by one of Mater Lachrymarum's henchmen using a sadistic tool seemingly designed for such a task.

The heady brew of violent and abhorrent sexual imagery on display in *Mother of Tears* is perhaps typified most obviously, and crudely, in the scene where Marta has a spear plunged into her body, through her genitalia and out of her mouth (mirroring Usher's dream-death in

Two Evil Eyes) in the ultimate penetration of phallic symbolism. This is repeated in somewhat more outrageous and outré proportions during the climax of the film when Mater Lachrymarum is impaled by a giant and elaborately ornate obelisk that has collapsed from the roof of the crumbling house. Like the other Mothers, Mater Lachrymarum's own house destroys her as it falls around her. Coincidently, the house used as the home of the Mother of Tears was also used to creepy effect in Mario Bava's *Kill Baby Kill* (1966).

When Sarah discovers the house of the Mother of Tears and ventures into the bowels of the building, she runs into a mass orgy of violence, ritualistic self-mutilation and sexual depravity, as the followers of the Third Mother indulge their darkest fantasies in scenes of abject degeneracy that would make Brian Yuzna blush.

The idea of witchcraft and its links to mental instability explored in *Suspiria* – particularly in the scene where Suzy meets Frank Mandel and he explains to her that 'bad luck isn't brought by broken mirrors, but by broken minds' – is revisited in this film too. Sarah Mandy believes she is experiencing a mental breakdown when the realisation of what is actually occurring around her sinks in. In a role that would appear to be the antithesis of his character in *Suspiria*, Udo Kier, here playing Father Johannes, informs Sarah that there is 'nothing wrong with your mind, it's the world that has gone crazy'.

Sarah spends much of the film trying to understand the ever-changing world around her. She is obsessed with her past and has never got over the death of her mother. The fact that she works in a museum demonstrates her firm-rootedness in the past and her links with a bygone era of alchemy and sorcery. Appearing childlike in the scenes where she is beseeching her mother to come back to her, Sarah is still a typical Argento heroine, strong willed and resourceful. This childlike slant is illustrated again in the fairytale-like exclamation by Mater Lachrymarum: 'Who wants to eat the girl?' This line was inspired by a nightmare Argento had of his headmistress trying to eat him as a boy. It is simple yet effective, preying on juvenile and primitive fears of cannibalism and heavy with fervent sexual undertones.

While we have the 'monstrous mother' in the shape of Mater Lachrymarum and the women who kill their young throughout the film, Argento for once also presents us with a protective and nurturing mother in the form of Elise Mandy. Contacting her mother from beyond the grave enables Sarah to hone her inherited powers. Her mother guides her throughout the film until she returns to the spirit world for good, dragging with her a minion of darkness tormenting Sarah. In another throwback to *Suspiria*, the minion pursuing Sarah is the reanimated corpse of her lover Michael, whose throat has been ripped out. This mirrors Sara's fate in *Suspiria* and, like her, Michael is not allowed to rest in peace, but is summoned to carry out the dark will of the Third Mother.

From the film's opening credits, Argento immediately references Renaissance paintings depicting all manner of eternal damnation, the occult and Christian interpretations of Hell and demonic atrocities. Extracts from Bosch's triptych 'The Garden of Earthly Delights' are included in this languid barrage of deviant and chilling imagery.

In one memorable scene, Argento even finds time to make a dig at Japanese horror cinema, and perhaps offer his own opinion on that subgenre's recent popularity and overkill. When the leader of the gaggle of witches (Jun Ichikawa) at the train station chases Sarah onto a train, she has her head busted open as Sarah repeatedly slams a door closed on it. Perhaps Argento is commenting that Italians still make the best horror movies? Argento's influence is indeed also evident in Japanese horror cinema. For instance, the supernatural entity stalking a loosely connected group of people in Takashi Shimizu's *Ju-On: The Grudge* (2003) is a mirror of events in *Inferno*. This director also pays homage, in the same film, to the taxi rides in *Suspiria* and *Inferno*.

Music

Simonetti provides an ominous score, much more subdued than those of *Suspiria* and *Inferno*. His restraint proves effective, though, and the film is significantly enhanced by his moody and brooding orchestrations. Gregorian chanting and sudden blasts of brass and strings immediately bring to mind Orff's *Carmina Burana* and Jerry Goldsmith's deeply sinister score for *The Omen*.

Verdict

Received with mixed reviews, *Mother of Tears* managed to defy everyone's expectations. Argento has delivered an engrossing and verging-on-camp horror-fest that is as outrageous and as over-the-top as you'd expect. While not quite the masterpiece fans would have hoped for, the film still marks Argento as a director who, even after all these years, follows his own vision and continues to explore the darkest recesses of his mind. While it fails to provide a worthy conclusion to the trilogy, as ever with Argento, it's the journey that is the important thing, not the destination. The bizarre spectacle of Sarah and Detective Marchi laughing uncontrollably against a matted background at the end would suggest that perhaps *Mother of Tears*, as deliriously over-the-top as it is, is Argento sending himself up. 'Carry on Grand Guignol', anyone?

Giallo (2009)

'Kiss kiss no more.'

Directed by: Dario Argento
Written by: Jim Agnew & Sean Keller
Executive Produced by: Donald A Barton, Adrien Brody, Aitana de Val, Luis de Val, Billy Dietrich, Patricia Eberle, Oscar Generale, Nesim Hason, John S Hicks, Lisa Lambert, Martin McCourt, David Milner
Music by: Marco Werba
Cinematography: Frederic Fasano
Edited by: Roberto Silvi
Production Designer: Davide Bassan
Cast: Adrien Brody (Inspector Enzo Avolfi), Emmanuelle Seigner (Linda),

Elsa Pataky (Celine), Robert Miano (Inspector Mori), Daniela Fazzolari (Sophia), Valentina Izumi (Keiko), Byron Deidra (Yellow)

Synopsis

When Celine, a beautiful model, goes missing after a fashion show, her sister Linda goes to the police. Eccentric Inspector Enzo Avolfi suspects that Celine may have been abducted by Yellow, an elusive serial killer – so called because of his jaundiced complexion, the result of a rare liver disease. Yellow has been abducting beautiful women from the streets of Turin and keeping them captive in his dank lair, torturing, horribly mutilating and eventually killing them. Enzo and Linda set out to find Celine before it is too late, but, before long, dark secrets from the past ominously surface and it seems Enzo, with his dubious motives, has more in common with Yellow than he would care to admit…

Background

Cameras began rolling on Argento's latest film in May 2008 in his favourite haunt, Turin. Perhaps because of the renewed interest in his work, possibly due to the highly anticipated conclusion of the 'Three Mothers' trilogy and the proposed remake of *Suspiria*, Argento returned once again to the genre in which he made his name.

Keller and Agnew wrote the screenplay in homage to the work of Argento. However, when they showed it to various studios in Hollywood, they realised how particular *giallo* films were to Italy: many producers had no concept of what the writers were trying to do. Keller stated: 'We both loved the *gialli* of the 60s and 70s and thought that a super-stylistic homage to the work of Argento, Bava and (Sergio) Martino would be a refreshing change to the horror scene. We wrote a script that was a kitchen-sink *giallo*. It had everything: opera, cats, black-gloved killers, flashbacks, red herrings, jazz, beautiful women dying horribly… We called it *Yellow*.'[12]

Eventually, Agnew passed the script on to a European producer who brought it to Argento. When he agreed to direct it, Argento worked closely with Keller and Agnew to tailor the script to his own taste. Aside from his *Masters of Horror* episodes, this film marked the first time that Argento had directed a film from a script other than his own, and even though the script was written in homage to his work, he was essentially a director for hire.

As well as a few familiar faces, the film also saw Argento working with some of the biggest names in Hollywood. Academy Award winner Adrien Brody was no stranger to the dark realms of horror cinema, having already appeared in titles such as *The Jacket* (2005) and *The Village* (2004). As well as amending the script, Brody was also an executive producer on *Giallo*. Emmanuelle Seigner's exotic and alluring features have graced such films as *The Ninth Gate* (1999) and *Frantic* (1988). Behind the camera, Argento was again joined by production designer Davide Bassan, who worked on *Opera* and *Suspiria* as an art director. *Giallo* was lensed by Argento's current regular cinematographer Frederic Fasano and special effects were once again provided by Sergio Stivaletti. The film's music was written and conducted by Spanish-born composer Marco Werba.

Giallo premiered at the Edinburgh International Film Festival in June 2009 and received rather lukewarm reviews.

Comments

Giallo is a blood-soaked love letter to the director's favourite titular subgenre and could very well introduce a whole new generation to the perverse charms of *gialli*. While arguably not an actual *giallo* film, *Giallo* unspools as a conventional thriller with an abundance of nods to Argento's back catalogue and is more a loving homage, playful parody and knowing throwback to the glorious heyday of the Italian *gialli*. The fact that Argento collaborated with American writers Jim Agnew and Sean Keller arguably suggests he was still keen to reach a wider audience with his work.

According to Keller, '*Giallo* brings up questions about masculinity and misogyny with a very pointed opinion. We've tackled religion and faith, karma, self-determination, existential angst, the high price of revenge, delusions of entitlement and the illusion of justice. These are the things that matter to us as writers and filmmakers. The fact that we weave these themes into a genre often maligned as idiotic or childish makes the process doubly pleasing.'[13]

Already a fan of Dario Argento's work, Keller claimed that the director had a huge influence on his writing. 'Argento's films balance the grisly and the beautiful in a way that knocks you off centre. The violence is always repellent and attractive at the same time, which causes a level of discomfort that heightens the horror.'[14]

Giallo is similar to recent works such as the *Masters of Horror* episodes, in that Argento wasn't solely responsible for the script, nor did he produce this film through his own company, Opera. One therefore wonders how much control the maestro held over his latest opus. Shortly after the premiere in Edinburgh, from which Argento was conspicuously absent, rumours began to abound that the director was unhappy with the final cut of the film, citing studio interference as the main cause of his discontent. Argento allegedly had problems with the film's producers as they attempted to influence and alter his creative vision – indeed, one glance at the number of people who produced *Giallo* would suggest that too many cooks do indeed spoil the broth. Speaking of the experience at a Fangoria convention in New York in June 2009, Argento stated that, as time went on, he lost more and more control over *Giallo* and that interference from US studio executives became too much for him. Allegedly, Argento also had problems when attempting to contact the producers after post-production with regard to the film's distribution. This echoes the similar experience he had whilst directing *Trauma* in the States.

It is obvious, however, that screenwriters Keller and Agnew are intimately familiar with Argento's work and, at times, *Giallo* is a melting pot of typically 'Argentoesque' moments and potently echoes much of the director's earlier work. Like *Phenomena*, *Trauma* and *Sleepless*, *Giallo* unfolds as a compilation of Argento's 'greatest hits' and revisits familiar themes and imagery. Much like everything else he has made since *Opera*, *Giallo* managed to subvert expectations and confound fans and critics alike.

Style/Technical

Giallo, like *The Card Player* and *Do You Like Hitchcock?*, exhibits none of Argento's directorial flair or panache, and instead illustrates a much more pared-down approach. Argento's camera is uncharacteristically restrained throughout proceedings; static even. It merely observes events from a safe distance rather than thrusting us into the midst of the ensuing chaos, which might be indicative of an objectivity on Argento's part towards material he wasn't responsible for writing.

Rather underwhelming direction aside, the film displays a similar look to much of his recent output, thanks to the seductive and wonderfully lush cinematography of Frederic Fasano, who also lensed *Do You Like Hitchcock?*, *Mother of Tears* and Asia Argento's *Scarlet Diva*.

While Argento's reputation has taken something of a battering during the last fifteen years or so, with the majority of his work panned by critics, it is quite evident that he still retains the ability to infuse astoundingly violent imagery with sexualised elegance and bizarre beauty. Even though *Giallo* is quite tame compared to most other Argento films, particularly its predecessor – the outrageously violent *Mother of Tears* – Argento has not completely lost his touch or his ability to shock. Though much of his direction in *Giallo* is toned down, he still directs the scenes of violence with inimitable vigour, particularly the grisly flashbacks which form some of the film's highlights. Indeed, the flashbacks depicting the demise of Enzo's mother – as the killer plunges a knife into her throat and mouth, mirroring the gory demise of Stefan in *Opera* – have a particularly oneiric tone and could reasonably fit into any number of Argento's previous films. In these blood-dark scenes, Argento achieves something more akin to what audiences are used to from him, with their warped vigour, distorted atmosphere and gently tilting camera combining to create imagery that is peculiarly hallucinatory. Another flashback, depicting an immensely violent and utterly intense confrontation between a young Enzo and his mother's killer, unfolds within the confines of a butcher's shop, with unforgettably brutal results.

As with *The Card Player*, Argento also displays what amounts to effective restraint in certain scenes throughout *Giallo*. Rather than show us everything, there are a number of shocking moments where he cuts away, leaving the rest to our imagination and thus heightening the effect. This is exemplified when Yellow takes a pair of pruning sheers to Keiko's lip. When he has gripped her lip with them and seems sure to snip, Argento immediately cuts and we are left with the nasty afterthought. This prompted at least one member of the audience at the premiere to beat a hasty retreat from the screening.

Argento, as always, makes excellent use of his location. Turin's breathtaking cityscape once more evokes a moody and grandiose atmosphere, as it did in *Deep Red* and *Sleepless*, with its old buildings and baroque architecture all harking back to the past – in much the same way as the film itself does in its homage to *giallo* films and Argento's earlier work.

Davide Bassan's production design simply exudes class and sophisticated elegance, from the strikingly chic fashion houses with their endless parades of impossibly glamorous models, to Celine's ornate apartment and Enzo's spacious office. Thanks to this and Fasano's stunning photography, the film retains an alluring and resplendent tone that is redolent of nothing short of high art.

The copious numbers of red objects that cut through the otherwise reservedly dark and sombre look of the film prove highly striking, from Enzo's shopping bag, to the pillars that line Yellow's creepy chambers, to the backdrop of the café where Enzo confides in Linda.

Not to mention, of course, the various scenes of bloody torture and murderous rampages.

Bassan imbues Yellow's lair with an unshakably seedy and grimy feel that contrasts remarkably with the 'outside' world that ostracises him. With all its exquisite beauty, it is representative of everything he is not.

Indeed, it is during these scenes that *Giallo* displays elements and imagery much more akin to visuals associated with various emergent films such as *Hostel* (2005) and *Captivity* (2007), which have been labelled by critics as 'torture porn'. Yellow's unsavoury hideout, with its cold, industrial demeanour and distressing-looking operating table – complete with blood-spattered and soiled restraints – is much more Eli Roth than Dario Argento. The moments featuring the torture of Keiko and Celine contain none of the opulence or aestheticism usually associated with Argento's particular brand of sadism. Argento himself has expressed varied opinions on 'torture porn' and this aspect of the film could perhaps be interpreted as his acknowledgement of filmmakers such as Eli Roth and James Wan, who have long cited Argento as a major influence on their film work.

The dialogue and its delivery is at times stilted and awkward, though this is far from unusual for an Argento film, as he prefers to concentrate on creating a specific mood and tone rather than coaxing effective performances from his actors.

Whilst *Giallo* opens with some quintessential 'Argentoesque' imagery, particularly the scene inside the opera house and the various shots of Yellow's eyes reflected in the rear-view mirror of his taxi, the film unfurls without his characteristic, gravity-defying camerawork. Also notably absent are the sinister point-of-view shots that usually serve to align us with the killer or the victim's line of sight. Aside from a few notably bizarre exceptions, such as the point-of-view shot of Yellow obsessively scrubbing himself with bleach and then bringing his hands up to the camera to sniff at them, events here are captured in a staunchly objective manner.

Themes

Giallo feels like a whirlwind tour of all-things-Argento. Many of the usual themes associated with the director's work are echoed throughout the film: the outsider protagonist, the destruction of beauty in the form of sexy female victims, lavishly filmed scenes of brutal violence, a villain with distinct psychosexual issues and revealing flashbacks that are woven into a twisting narrative. In keeping with the traditional investigations carried out in any number of *gialli*, clues are often simply stumbled upon or plucked from the air moments before another audacious plot twist occurs and we are yanked along by the story to its next grisly instalment.

Giallo doesn't serve as a deconstruction of the genre like *Tenebrae* and, to a lesser extent, *Sleepless* – it is more a knowing parody of *giallo* films.

While much of Argento's later output has been fairly self-referential, particularly *Sleepless* and *Do You Like Hitchcock?*, his films have always expressed an undeniable cine-literacy – even the screenplays he wrote for other directors at the beginning of his career exhibited an intimate understanding of cinema. *Giallo* seems to be the rational culmination of this self-awareness and, like *Phenomena*, *Trauma* and *Sleepless* before it, it acts as a kind of melting pot of Argento moments, celebrating his cinematic heritage.

The title of the film not only refers to the titular villain's skin colour, but also to the genre itself. This self-referential approach was praised by most critics, although some found it hard to fathom. As mentioned, Argento has often referenced the work of other directors in his films, usually to enhance certain nuances or subtexts within his own narratives.

Despite the wealth of reflexivity that exists in the film, Argento apparently didn't want to appear too self-referential, which is odd considering the concept of the script was to pay homage to the genre he helped create.

A number of cuts were made by the director, and amongst these was the removal of the traditional *giallo* villain garb of dark leather raincoat, fedora and black leather gloves – instead, Yellow stumbles around in a hooded jacket and headband. Nevertheless, the resulting film still displays a playful tone rife with sly nods to past favourites.

A particularly glorious homage to *Opera* occurs when Yellow confronts Linda at Celine's apartment. Enzo is in the hallway on the other side of the front door and looks through the peephole. We are immediately reminded of the scene in *Opera* where Betty's assistant makes the same mistake and ends up getting shot in the eye and hurled back down the corridor in graceful slow motion. As Enzo stares through the peephole, Yellow points a gun to it, and we are once again reminded that the act of looking is still just as dangerous in a contemporary Argento thriller as it was in his earlier work.

The climactic rooftop chase, featuring the murderer plunging to his death from a great height, echoes the climax of *Cat O'Nine Tails*. Yellow clutches wildly at anything that may save him from falling, and, like Casoni clutching at the elevator cords and burning his hands in *Cat*, gropes at a window frame encrusted with broken glass. When he falls through the glass roof below, one can't help but remember Pat's sadistic murder at the beginning of *Suspiria* as her body also bursts through ornate glass and is cut to ribbons.

When Linda finds a digital video camera containing footage of Celine begging for mercy, images from *The Card Player* are instantly evoked. *Giallo* is also similar to *The Card Player* in that its narrative proceeds like that of a conventional detective thriller, following events from the point of view of the police, rather than the amateur sleuths of earlier Argento films.

The deadly taxi rides that various characters take throughout the story recall those much more nightmarishly unnerving journeys in *Suspiria*, *Inferno* and *Mother of Tears*.

When Celine escapes from the confines of Yellow's underground lair and emerges into the outside world, she allows herself but a brief second of euphoric respite before continuing with her attempt to escape. She touches a nearby tree leaf in a moment that tenderly recalls Betty's absorption into nature at the end of *Opera*. The moment, while rather absurd, is strangely poetic.

The ambiguous and rather bleak ending echoes that of *Cat O'Nine Tails* as we find ourselves wondering what Celine's fate will be as her cries for help go unheard by the inept security guard. The last shot, lingering on a pool of blood forming beneath the trunk of the car where she is bound and gagged, mirrors the last shot of *Deep Red*, as a devastated and traumatised Marc gazes into the red depths, awestruck by the preceding events. It also serves to highlight the fact that Celine's time is rapidly running out.

Argento also finds time to reference the work of another artist he admires in the scene where Enzo purchases a book by Japanese photographer Nobuyoshi Araki, famed for his edgy and erotic images of the female body.

The seemingly random and often strange clues to the killer's identity found in Argento's other films (clues provided by paintings, mirrors, whispers and half-glimpsed truths), are echoed here, to some degree, in Enzo's recognition of an old company logo that reveals Yellow's whereabouts. However, this visual clue lacks the abstract mystery of previous 'Argentoesque' clues. Another clue is provided by Keiko, who whispers the word 'yellow' before she dies.

In the background of one scene is a poster of Sergio Leone's *The Good, the Bad and the Ugly* (1966), stirring memories of Argento's early days as a writer of various westerns and his work with Leone. This playfulness is also apparent when Enzo and Linda walk past a poster advertising *Juno* (2007) – a film in which the title character discusses the merits of Dario Argento and how he is a much better 'master of horror' than Herschell Gordon Lewis.

One of the defining characteristics of *gialli* is their stylish depiction of the destruction of beauty, and this concept provides the motives for the grisly actions of the eponymous villain in *Giallo*. He resents anything beautiful and seeks to destroy it, deliberately mutilating his attractive victims and bundling their bodies up in bubble wrap, as if to morbidly highlight their beautiful and all-too-mortal fragility. The idea of a beautiful model in danger recalls the glamorous and imperilled world of high fashion as depicted in Mario Bava's groundbreaking *Blood and Black Lace* (1964). Linda's occupation as an air steward-ess is one that, prior to the days of budget airlines, evoked a touch of glamour and chic and also fits into the idea of elevated beauty.

Yellow photographs his victims as he tortures and mutilates them, his glee at capturing their petrified features recalling Berti's similar actions during his killing spree in *Tenebrae*. This preoccupa-tion with the gaze and modes of visual communication is a common thread that weaves its way through Argento's oeuvre. The photos that adorn the walls of Enzo's office all exhibit the destruction of beauty and serve to highlight this obsession of Argento's, forming a grotesque and striking gallery of violence and death. This use of the camera to capture violent and shocking imagery, and revel in sadistic mayhem, is much like what Argento uses his own camera for.

In the original screenplay, Yellow cut off the eyelids of his victims before forcing them to look at their disfigured reflections in a mirror. Had it remained in the film, this would have echoed the central idea of *Opera* – the concept of someone unable to look away and being forced to gaze at spectacles of terror and anguish, a notion that typi-fies Argento's work.

Another recurring motif of Argento's that is evident in *Giallo* is that of eye violation. When Celine is abducted by Yellow, he injects her with a tranquiliser in the corner of her eye, but not before sadisti-cally taunting her by holding the needle in front of her eyes. Various close-up shots of eyes with sharp implements advancing towards them reappear throughout the film.

The psychological trauma of various characters in previous films such as *The Bird with the Crystal Plumage*, *Four Flies on Grey Velvet*, *Deep Red*, *Phenomena*, *Opera* and *Trauma* is present here, too, in the form of Yellow, a hideously disfigured and warped individual. His hatred of beauty stems from his sordid and tragic past – his mother was a drug-addled whore who abandoned him at birth. Brought up in the strict confines of a convent, he was dubbed Yellow by his cruel peers due to his jaundiced skin. Ostracised from society, his pain and hatred was left to fester. In a bizarre twist of casting, Adrien Brody, under the pseudonymous moniker of Byron Deidra, also portrays the utterly unhinged Yellow. Under a hefty layer of prosthetics, the actor does his best to make the killer as vile and repugnant as he can – at one stage Yellow is glimpsed sucking on a child's pacifier and masturbating whilst gazing at photographs of his disfigured victims.

As the film progresses, Yellow becomes increasingly pathetic, particularly in light of his tragic childhood. Ultimately, though, the villain is one of Argento's weakest and comes across as a ridiculous pantomime character, resembling a latex caricature.

The psychological trauma is not just reserved for the disturbed killer, however; the tortured Enzo also has a dark and troubling past from which he cannot escape. Enzo is a somewhat typical Argento protagonist. An outsider, self-destructive, untrusting and a total loner, Enzo grew up in America after witnessing his mother's death at the hands of a sadistic killer. As a young man, he returned to Italy and sought revenge, eventually being taken under the wing of Inspector Mori. Enzo understands how the killer thinks – but he would rather kill Yellow than trust him to reveal Celine's whereabouts. Throughout the course of the film, various similarities between Enzo and Yellow are revealed: both are outcasts, have traumatic memories of childhood and 'mother' issues, and both have been relegated to their respective underground bases. At the end of the film, Linda hurls abuse at Enzo, screaming 'You're just like him!'

Enzo lives, works and exists pretty much alone. Utterly consumed by his job, the shot of a bed in his office suggests that there is nothing more to him than his work and highlights just how out of step with contemporary society he is.

He is quite similar to Michael Brandon's Roberto Tobias in *Four Flies* and is rather unsympathetic, particularly at the film's climax when his dark and selfish agenda is swiftly and mercilessly executed.

The relationship between Enzo and Linda recalls similar detective/
novice pairings in *Deep Red*, *Sleepless* and *Cat O'Nine Tails*. Linda
is a typical Argento female – strong willed and determined. The icily
detached performance from Seigner recalls similar performances
from several of Argento's other leading ladies, particularly Cristina
Marsillach and Catherine Spaak.

Giallo is an indictment of the machismo that pervades most cop
thrillers, and indeed horror films, in that it is not sufficient to merely
apprehend and imprison the villain, or save the life of a victim; you
must adhere to archaic, Old Testament-styled blood justice and kill
the bad guy. *Giallo* presents resourceful women (no strangers to
Argento's narratives) who might have saved themselves had it not
been for the interference of Enzo, a reckless cop with an agenda of
his own. This forms a direct response to the misogyny which *giallo*
films, and indeed Argento's collective works, are often accused of.
Celine and Linda are similar to Suzy, Jennifer, Betty and Anna Mari
in that they are resilient enough to try and do whatever it takes to
ensure their own survival. In *Giallo*, it is a man – Enzo – who scup-
pers their plans and possibly ensures Celine's demise. Enzo believes
the only way to stop Yellow is to kill him. Aside from *Opera* perhaps,
most of Argento's villains are shown no mercy when it comes to
their respective denouements.

The Motor Vehicle Registration bureaucrat obsessed with Westerns and the drool pathologist provide the film with some suitably
dark humour and recall the various other quirky minor characters
from the likes of *Cat O'Nine Tails* and *Four Flies on Grey Velvet*.
The scene featuring Enzo and the pathologist simultaneously lighting cigarettes and smoking whilst performing an autopsy is grimly
humorous. In yet another 'Argentoesque' case of art imitating life,
Adrien Brody and Elsa Pataky were a couple whilst filming *Giallo*:
one can't help but be reminded of Argento's onscreen torture of his
former partner and, indeed, his daughters throughout the years.

Music

Argento turned to composer Marco Werba to score *Giallo*. No stranger to orchestrating music to accompany disturbing and graphic imagery, Werba has composed scores for a number of highly atmospheric independent horror films, such as Ivan Zuccon's HP Lovecraft adaptation *Colour from the Dark* (2008) and *giallo* throwback *Darkness Surrounds Roberta* (2008).

Adrien Brody was sent a few samples of Werba's previous work and was so impressed he immediately recommended the musician to Argento.

Werba composed a grand and sweepingly haunting orchestral score akin to Bernard Herrmann's work, as he believed Argento's latest film was in a similar vein to the films of Hitchcock and Brian De Palma. Werba commented: 'I thought that *Giallo* was a classic thriller and needed symphonic music. As much as I like the previous compositions by Goblin for the likes of *Profondo Rosso* and *Suspiria*, I thought that sort of style would not fit the mood of *Giallo*. The music of *Giallo* is completely different from the previous scores of Argento films.'[15]

Conducting the Bulgarian Symphony Orchestra, Werba has created a darkly dramatic, beautifully foreboding and utterly appropriate score for Argento's film. Ominously swirling strings and spooky choral arrangements stabbed at by a blasting brass section collide to provide one of the film's undisputed highlights. Werba effortlessly evokes the likes of Bernard Herrmann and, indeed, Danny Elfman while still imbuing his score with a distinct and unique grandeur all of its own.

Verdict

Structured around various gory set pieces, *Giallo* unfolds with a much more concise and conventional narrative than any other Argento film and an engaging momentum is sustained throughout. While it lacks the abstract visuals and stunning camerawork that populates so much of his earlier output, it still proves to be an arresting-looking and thoroughly entertaining film. At times verging on camp, but always knowingly so, it reveals a more playful side to Argento. The screenplay by Keller and Agnew unfolds as a fond homage to a genre they obviously revere and a director they have the utmost respect for. Despite the problematic post-production, Argento devotees might still find much to admire in *Giallo*.

Trivia

Vincent Gallo, Ray Liotta and Asia Argento were initially linked to the film; however, one by one, they backed out, in Gallo's case allegedly due to 'creative differences' with his ex, Asia, who ironically left the production a little later to work on Alejandro Jodorowsky's *King Shot* (2009) and have a baby.

ARTISTIC ARTERIES: ARGENTO'S WORK AS PRODUCER

'There's some kind of madman loose in here!'

Dawn of the Dead (1978)

Directed/Written/Edited by: George A Romero
Producer/Script Consultant/Music: Dario Argento
Produced by: Claudio Argento & Richard P Rubinstein
Music by: Goblin
Cinematographer: Michael Gornick
Production Designer: Josie Caruso & Barbara Lifsher
Special Effects: Tom Savini
Cast: David Emge (Stephen), Gaylen Ross (Francine), Ken Foree (Peter), Scott H Reiniger (Roger), David Crawford (Dr Foster), David Early (Mr Berman)
Also known as: *Zombi, Dawn of the Living Dead, Zombies*

Synopsis

Following an ever-increasing pandemic of the dead returning to life and devouring the living, a small band of survivors seek refuge in a shopping mall. Fortifying the place, they believe they can wait there until they are rescued. Events take a turn for the worse, however, when their sanctuary is pillaged by malevolent humans, and the group soon realise they have more to worry about than the marauding zombies outside...

Comments

Being a huge fan of *Night of the Living Dead* (1968), Argento was interested in working with George Romero, especially after a mutual friend showed him the script of Romero's proposed follow-up to *Night of the Living Dead: Dawn of the Dead.* Argento used his European connections and influence to help secure funding for the project. When Romero travelled to Italy to meet with Argento, it was the beginning of a beautiful, albeit blood-drenched friendship, though the two men couldn't have been more different, personally or artistically. This would become more apparent on their second and weakest collaboration, *Two Evil Eyes.*

Argento was so enthusiastic about *Dawn of the Dead* that he apparently travelled around the Caribbean researching Haitian lore and voodoo. Shooting began in November 1977, prior to Argento filming *Inferno.*

Argento worked as a script consultant on the film and any changes to the script were okayed by him. The two men never clashed and Argento had the good sense to leave Romero to direct the film, fully trusting him to deliver the goods. Indeed, Argento was so respectful to Romero that he only visited the set once, preferring to let the director work without having a producer breathing down his neck. Similarly, Romero was obviously savvy enough and trusted Argento with the final cut of certain versions of the film. Argento also rounded up the members of Goblin and collaborated on the eerily droning soundtrack that is one of the genre's most defining pieces of music.

Dawn of the Dead premiered in Italy a whole six months before it screened in the States and was renamed *Zombi.* Its success in Europe played a huge part in Romero securing a distribution deal in America. Romero allowed Argento the final cut of the film in the European, non-English-language versions. Argento believed that the violence and moodiness of the film didn't lend itself to comic moments. He removed several comedic moments, resulting in a film with a darker edge. He also personally directed the actors providing the dubbing for the Italian version and mixed the soundtrack himself.

The success of *Dawn of the Dead* (as is quite typical in the film industry) led to a slew of imitations and rip-offs, most notably from band-wagon jumper Lucio Fulci, who devised his script for *Zombi 2* aka *Zombie Flesh Eaters* (1979) to cash in on the success of Romero and Argento's effort. The dastardly duo planned to embark on a sequel together and co-wrote a treatment for *Day of the Dead* (1985), but plans were shelved due to the subsequent erupting zombie fad. When Romero came to direct this film a few years later, Argento had to bow out of the collaboration due to the unfavourable strength of the dollar against the lira.

Demoni/Demons (1985)

Directed/Written by: Lamberto Bava
Written/Produced by: Dario Argento
Co-written by: Franco Ferrini
Story by: Dardano Sacchetti
Cinematography: Gianlorenzo Battaglia
Edited by: Piero Bozza & Franco Fraticelli
Production Designer: Davide Bassan
Special Effects: Sergio Stivaletti
Cast: Natasha Hovey (Cheryl), Urbano Barberini (George), Paola Cozzo (Kathy), Karl Zinny (Ken), Fiore Argento (Hannah), Nicoletta Elmi (Ingrid)

Synopsis

A group of people invited to the premiere of a mysterious horror movie become trapped in the cinema. One of the patrons becomes a bloodthirsty, fanged demon after scratching her face on a mask in the foyer and she attacks the other people. One by one they are infected and transform into vicious fiends. The remaining survivors try to survive the night while looking for a way out of the building.

Comments

After the negative reception of *Phenomena*, Argento decided to take a brief hiatus from directing and chose to allow his creativity to breathe by producing a couple of films for his friend Lamberto Bava, son of Mario Bava. Bava had worked with Argento on several of his films as an assistant director. He also worked with his father, co-directing much of Mario's last film, *Shock* (1977), starring Daria Nicolodi, as his father was ill. A few of his own early directorial efforts received favourable reviews, such as *A Blade in the Dark* (1983) and *Macabre* (1980). Argento formed a new production company called DAC to keep himself occupied while his father retired and his brother worked on other projects. The idea for *Demons* was conceived by Dardano Sacchetti as the first film in a trilogy tracking the exploits of the titular creatures. Together with Lamberto Bava and Franco Ferrini, Argento wrote a script for the film that was inspired by social anxiety at the time. The 'video-nasty' era was in full-blooded bloom and critics lambasted horror films, holding them responsible for civil unrest and violent outbursts in the wider community.

Ditching plans to film in England, Argento favoured the stark coldness of Berlin for many of the exterior scenes, while the interior scenes were filmed in the De Paolis Studio in Rome. With a budget of $1.8 million, *Demons* was released in 1985 and went on to break box-office records in Europe and abroad.

Incorporating ideas from all three instalments of the planned trilogy, *Demons* has at its core an exploration of the alleged relationship between cinematic violence and its audience. A quintessential Italian horror film, it shamelessly references the work of Argento and Mario Bava, from its lighting and ear-splitting soundtrack, through its distinct lack of logic and coherence, to its savage and nightmarish imagery depicting all manner of gastric-churning violence.

While much of the cast were unfamiliar to audiences at the time, a number of them would go on to work with Argento again (though, in the case of his daughter Fiore, this would take years, as the experience proved most unpleasant for the aspiring actress-turned-fashion designer). Michele Soavi, who would later direct *The Church* and *The Sect*, plays the mysterious masked man who gives the girls complimentary tickets for the horror movie premiere at the beginning of the film. Soavi was no stranger to acting, having appeared in Argento's *Phenomena*, *City of the Living Dead* (1980) and his own directorial debut *Stage Fright* (1987), as a James Dean-obsessed cop.

Nowadays the film has garnered a strong cult following and it is favoured by audiences who hold a 'so-bad-it's-good' inclination. The flimsy characters, ludicrous dialogue and daft plotting are all overshadowed by the film's *raison d'être*: its absurdly graphic and splashy special effects, once again courtesy of Sergio Stivaletti.

Trivia

The part of the blind man was written with Vincent Price in mind.

Demoni 2/Demons 2 (1986)

Directed/Written by: Lamberto Bava
Written/Produced by: Dario Argento
Co-written by: Franco Ferrini
Story by: Dardano Sacchetti
Music by: Simon Boswell
Cinematographer: Gianlorenzo Battaglia
Edited by: Piero Bozza
Production Designer: Davide Bassan
Special Effects: Sergio Stivaletti & Danilo Bollettini
Cast: David Edwin Knight (George), Nancy Brilli (Hannah), Coralina Cataldi-Tassoni (Sally), Asia Argento (Ingrid), Marco Vivio (Tommy), Lorenzo Gioielli (Jake)
Also known as: *Demons 2: The Nightmare Returns*

Synopsis

During her birthday celebrations, Sally is attacked by a demon that emerges from her television set as she watches a horror film, transforming her into a hideous, toothy monster. Attacking her party guests, she infects them, turning them into ferocious demons too. Trapped in the high-rise apartment building, the other residents soon fall prey to the marauding beasts as they attempt to flee for their lives.

Comments

The success of the first film ensured a follow-up and, as the initial idea was to create a trilogy, Argento and Bava gleefully began filming in May 1986 in Rome. *Demons 2* is essentially a remake of *Demons*. The cinema featured in the first film is here substituted with a swanky high-rise apartment block, à la *Shivers* (1975).

More references to the work of David Cronenberg come via the emergence of a malevolent entity through a television set, reminiscent of *Videodrome* (1983). As in that film, *Demons 2* also features a mysterious and potentially deadly broadcasting studio that is somehow responsible for unleashing the demons into everyday reality. While *Demons* vaguely commented on the notion that there was a distinct relationship between violence in horror films and audiences, the social criticism here is firmly levelled at television broadcasters, with the danger literally crawling out of a TV set. This idea would also be explored by Hideo Nakata in his groundbreaking *Ringu* (1998).

A voiceover reminiscent of those used in *Suspiria*, *Inferno*, *Phenomena* and *Phantom of the Opera* links events about to unfold in *Demons 2* to those of *Demons*. However, whereas the snippets of narration lent those former films a distinct fairytale quality, the same can't really be said of this rather pointless bout of exposition.

Bava and Argento have constructed *Demons 2* as a deliberate shock machine, purposefully setting up scenarios and building tension that eventually leads to the inevitable climax of blood-soaked chaos. The 'mechanics' of terror are extremely obvious and, though this film lacks the atmospheric touches of the original, it's not without a few similar memorable moments, such as the scene where Sally enters the darkened room and slowly approaches her birthday cake, its candles and the light from the room behind her giving the scene an eerie and suspenseful quality. Coralina Cataldi-Tassoni would appear in a number of Argento's later films and her death in *Mother of Tears* is one of Argento's most memorable and shocking. The script is surely one of Argento's most plodding and predictable, but that didn't stop *Demons 2* from being a huge hit. *Demons 2* has a surprisingly good soundtrack that utilises tracks by artists such as Dead Can Dance, The Cult, Art of Noise and The Smiths.

Like its predecessor, it also references moments from Argento's back catalogue and a few Mario Bava films too, such as *Kill Baby Kill* (1966), which is echoed in a creepy scene involving a child and a ball bouncing down an empty hallway.

This marked the last time Bava would work with Argento as he preferred henceforward to forge ahead with his own career, out of the formidable shadow of his former mentor. After a promising start to his career, Bava soon spiralled into television-orientated projects and the odd fantasy-adventure flick.

Trivia

Lamberto Bava cameos as Sally's father.

Giallo: La tua impronta del venerdi – TV Series (1987)

Created by: Enzo Tortora & Anna Tortora
Written by: Laura Grimaldi, Marco Tropea & Dardano Sacchetti
Produced by: Dario Argento
Music by: Manuel De Sica
Cinematographer: Angelo Pacchetti
Presented by: Enzo Tortora, Dario Argento & Alba Parietti
Cast of Turno di notte/Nightshift: Antonella Vitale (Calypso 9), Matteo Gazzolo (Rosso 27), Franco Cerri (Tango 28), Lea Martino (Loredana, the radio operator)

Dario Argento co-hosted and produced a magazine-format, prime-time TV show shortly after the release of *Opera*, during what was perhaps the peak of his success. This, his second foray into the realm of television, was broadcast from October 1987 until January 1988 and received mixed reviews, running for only one series.

The show had three main segments and Argento was the creative consultant on the latter two.

Giallo: the bracketing segment included live interviews with people involved in the film industry, specifically those involved in making *giallo* movies, and the fans of these films. During this segment, Argento would also reveal the secrets behind various special effects used in his films. Discussion panels and a quiz also took place where viewers and audience members could attempt to guess the identity of the killers in the short films from the third segment.

Gli incubi de Dario Argento/Dario Argento's Nightmares: the part of the show when Argento would introduce a three-minute short film he had written and directed himself. The shorts had no plots to speak of and were more a series of exercises in atmosphere, gruesome special effects and suspense. They featured all manner of bizarre and intense imagery (for a primetime TV show, this really cut close to the bone), including murder, cannibalism and rape. Argento co-introduced these films, in a devilishly enthusiastic fashion, with Coralina Cataldi-Tassoni. These films have more in common with those that Argento produced for others, such as *Demons*, etc, and don't really resemble the director's usual style.

Turno di notte/Nightshift: a series of short films directed by Luigi Cozzi and Lamberto Bava lasting 20 minutes each. Each episode boasted guest actors including Daria Nicolodi, Asia Argento, Mirella D'Angelo (*Tenebrae*) and Maria Chiara Sasso (*Demons 2*). The episodes were linked by recurring characters who worked for the mysterious Calypso Taxis, including Antonella Vitale (*Opera*) and Lea Martino from Lamberto Bava's *You'll Die at Midnight* (1986). Viewers were invited to guess the identity of the killer in each instalment. Argento was also creative consultant of this segment.

The latter two segments were pre-filmed and Argento's involvement was more pronounced in these. His role in the show secured it media exposure and guaranteed shock value.

La chiesa/The Church (1989)

Directed/Written by: Michele Soavi
Written/Produced by: Dario Argento
Co-written by: Franco Ferrini
Music by: Keith Emerson & Philip Glass
Cinematographer: Renato Tafuri
Edited by: Franco Fraticelli
Production Designer: Antonello Geleng
Special Effects: Sergio Stivaletti
Cast: Barbara Cupisti (Lisa), Hugh Quarshie (Father Gus), Asia Argento (Lotte), Tomas Arana (Evan), Feodor Chaliapin Jr (The Bishop), Giovanni Lombardo Radice (Reverend)
Also known as: *Demons 3, In the Land of the Demons, Demon Cathedral*

Synopsis

In medieval times, the Templar Knights exterminate the inhabitants of a quiet village accused of devil worship. Their bodies are buried in mass graves, above which a colossal church is built.

Flash forward to the present day when the opening of a sealed crypt in the basement of the church seals shut the only exit, trapping a group of tourists, historians and clergy inside the building. The spirits of the dead beneath the church begin possessing the people trapped inside and a small group of survivors must figure out a way to escape and stop the evil that lurks in the building from getting out.

Comments

The Church was intended as the third instalment of the proposed *Demons* trilogy. It is very loosely based on a short story by MR

James entitled *The Treasure of Abbot Thomas*, about a historian who finds a clue to hidden treasures in a stained-glass window. Bava was set to direct but the studio were unhappy with this decision as most of his output at the time was limited to TV movies. Argento turned, a little begrudgingly, to Soavi, another protégé who had worked as an assistant director for him on several films. Soavi had previously directed the above average and highly stylised slasher flick *Stage Fright* and incurred the wrath of Argento when he declined to work on the TV series *Giallo: La tua impronta del venerdi*, choosing instead to work with Terry Gilliam on *The Adventures of Baron Munchausen* (1988). As soon as the two reconciled and Soavi became involved in the project, it was clear he didn't want this film to be associated with the *Demons* films; instead, he wanted to branch out and make his own mark with it and insisted upon a number of changes. Argento relented and the two compromised. Indeed, while the film is indelibly 'Argentoesque', Soavi makes an ambitious attempt to explore themes and ideas that concern him. *The Church* marked his continuation, after *Stage Fright*, of the exploration of his own visual style that is also evident in his later films, *The Sect* and *Dellamorte Dellamore* aka *Cemetery Man* (1994).

The film was shot in Rome, Hamburg and Budapest, where the cathedral was situated.

With its convoluted and wandering plot, religious imagery and symbolism, shocking violence and lashings of creepy atmosphere, it is easy to see Argento's influence on *The Church*. The mechanics behind the devices used to seal the door of the church recall similar imagery used in *Inferno*, while the Gothic and damned church at the centre of the story recalls similarly damned buildings in the 'Three Mothers' trilogy.

Soavi seems to have absorbed Argento's use of astounding set pieces and the film is structured around these. A number of them are visually breathtaking, such as the exploration of the basement and the discovery of the broken seal, causing the floor to drop away, leaving an eerily glowing hole shaped like a crucifix. Soavi also appears to have been heavily influenced by Mario Bava and Riccardo Freda, particularly in his use of symbolism and visual allegories.

The opening scenes of the film feature the bloody massacre of an entire village by the Templar Knights, vaguely recalling the spectral knights of the *Blind Dead* (1971–75) films by Amando de Ossorio. The director also finds time to reference the likes of *The Shining* (1980) and *Rosemary's Baby* (1968) in a number of scenes. Soavi employs Argento's painterly touch in a number of scenes too, referencing works of art, as exemplified in the strangely sensual scene where the biker's naked girlfriend is embraced by a winged demon, an amalgamation of John Collier's 'Lilith' and a number of paintings by Boris Vallejo. Similarly, a number of Sergio Stivaletti's creature effects were inspired by the work of comic-book artist Vallejo, including the bizarre sea-creature that lunges at the bridegroom from the holy water font.

While Soavi has arguably absorbed his mentor's visual style, it is obvious he is an accomplished director in his own right. The film is laced with sinister yet deeply alluring imagery, such as the bridal gown caught in the locked door, shown from the outside of the building, fluttering hauntingly in the wind. There are also a number of strange and disturbing dream sequences in which Soavi really lets rip with the grotesque imagery, such as when the bridal model begins clawing her own face off while gazing into a mirror. The score, provided by Keith Emerson and Philip Glass, is suitably foreboding and enhances the graphic proceedings effectively.

La setta/The Sect (1991)

Directed/Written by: Michele Soavi
Written/Produced by: Dario Argento
Co-written by: Giovanni Romoli
Music by: Pino Donaggio
Cinematographer: Raffaele Mertes

Edited by: Franco Fraticelli
Production Designer: Antonello Geleng
Special Effects: Sergio Stivaletti & Massimo Cristofanelli
Cast: Kelly Curtis (Miriam), Herbert Lom (Moebius Kelly), Maria Angela Giordano (Kathryn), Michel Adatte (Frank), Carla Cassola (Dr Pernath), Angelika Maria Boeck (Claire), Giovanni Lombardo Radice (Martin)
Also known as: *The Devil's Daughter*, *Demons 4*

Synopsis

Frankfurt, Germany. School teacher Miriam narrowly avoids driving over an old man carrying a box in the middle of the road. She reluctantly agrees to take him home with her and soon realises that their meeting was not accidental. It transpires that the man is Moebius Kelly, an elder of a satanic sect that has been awaiting signs from the cosmos which will reveal who the bearer of Satan's child is to be: Miriam.

Comments

The Sect is another occult offering from Soavi and Argento and was the amalgamation of two separate scripts: *The Well* by Soavi and *Catacombs* by Giovanni Romali. As well as co-writing the script, Argento also created the disturbing prologue set in the desert and involving the massacre of a hippy commune by a crazed cult leader. Soavi's usual visual flourishes make a welcome return and really benefit from the tight plot and attention paid to the script. As a result, the director's fluid camerawork, striking set design and dreamy atmospherics all pivot on a riveting story about an ordinary young woman thrust into an extraordinary and disturbing situation. What makes it even more involving is the truly startling performance from Kelly Curtis, sister of Jamie Lee Curtis.

After seeing exactly what Soavi was capable of when he directed *The Church*, Argento was extremely supportive of his novice during the filming of *The Sect* and was careful not to put pressure on the young director, having enough faith in him to allow him to breathe.

Soavi, having learned a great deal from working with Argento on *The Church*, didn't feel threatened when he visited the set.

Like *Suspiria*, *Inferno* and *Phenomena* before it, *The Sect* is a dreamy fantasy-horror, deeply influenced by fairytales and mythology, particularly the feverish writings of Lewis Carroll. The film has a strange, otherworldly atmosphere soaked in the very stuff of nightmares. Strange pollen billows through the air in many scenes, highlighting the stifling and dreamlike environment the characters wander through. Soavi imbues events with a heady mix of druid and Celtic iconography and symbolism.

There are also a number of moments that defy logic or explanation, such as Miriam's pet rabbit turning on a television set and flicking through the channels!

Of course, this being an Argento production, the film is not without its violent set pieces, such as the scenes involving the mutilation of Kathryn at the hands of a possessed truck driver, her subsequent efflorescence of blood all over the hospital and a woman having her face ripped off under the spooky light of a full moon. Several creepy dream sequences permeate the film, including one involving Miriam wandering through a field towards a tree hanging with wind chimes and disturbing trinkets, only to be molested by a humanoid creature with the head of a giant bird.

There are a few sly nods to Argento's work here too, notably when a seemingly possessed man shoots himself and blood sprays onto a painting behind him, and in the scene where Miriam is administering eye drops in uncomfortable close-up, echoing darker deeds done to eyes in Argento's films. As in *Inferno*, water takes on decidedly sinister undertones: the well in Miriam's basement acts as a gateway to hell, allowing Soavi to fully explore his fondness for subterranean locations, dripping with Freudian connotations. In an eerily serene scene, Miriam is lowered into it as it will be used as her birthing pool, and creepy nursemaids surface from the ethereal blue depths like brides of Dracula.

The Sect is a slow-burning, taut and surreal experience, doused in religious metaphor and unforgettable imagery. It is easy to become immersed in the story as Miriam frantically flees from the cult, becoming paranoid and not knowing who she can trust, Soavi's camera prowling after her all the while, lapping up every sinister detail of his *Rosemary's Baby* on acid.

MDC Maschera di cera/The Wax Mask (1997)

Directed by: Sergio Stivaletti
Story/Produced by: Dario Argento
Written by: Lucio Fulci & Daniele Stroppa
Music by: Maurizio Abeni
Cinematographer: Sergio Salvati
Edited by: Paolo Benassi
Production Designer: Antonello Geleng
Special Effects: Sergio Stivaletti
Cast: Robert Hossein (Boris Volkoff), Romina Mondello (Sonia Lafont), Riccardo Serventi Longhi (Andrea), Gabriella Giorgelli (Aunt Francesca), Umberto Balli (Alex), Valery Valmond (Giorgina)

Synopsis

Paris, 1900. Young Sonia witnesses a masked man with a metal-clawed hand mutilate her parents and rip out their still-beating hearts. Twelve years later, Sonia is living in Rome with her blind aunt. She is hired as a dressmaker in a new waxworks museum owned by the mysterious Volkoff, notorious for his lifelike recreations of ghastly murder scenes. A recent spate of gruesome murders in Rome leads journalist Andrea to the museum. He and Sonia begin to suspect a disturbing connection between the deaths and the new, strangely familiar, wax figures appearing in the halls of the museum.

Comments

The Wax Mask was initially conceived as a collaboration between Dario Argento and Lucio Fulci. The two were rivals and Argento always felt that Fulci ripped off much of his work. When they met at a film festival in Rome in 1994, however, Argento was genuinely shocked and upset to see Fulci, now in the depths of ill health, arrive in a wheelchair. He suggested to Fulci that they make something together and Fulci, who had become much less prolific than previously, gratefully accepted. Scrapping plans to remake *The Mummy* (1932), they eventually decided to film Gaston Leroux's tale *The Wax Museum*. Fulci was keen to let the film play out as a Gothic romance and Argento insisted on sublime violence. Tragically, Fulci died before filming commenced. Argento paid for his funeral as a mark of respect and, after waiting for a time, decided to hand the reins of the project to his special-effects man, Sergio Stivaletti. This would be Stivaletti's directorial debut and, with Argento by his side, he felt confident.

The film is a throwback to vintage horrors of old, but like Argento's own *Phantom of the Opera*, possesses a strange, postmodern edge. Shot in Italy in July 1996 with a budget of $3 million, *The Wax Mask* boasts grand and lavish set design and desperately aims to reach the Gothic heights of the films of Mario Bava. Stivaletti doesn't quite possess the same visual finesse as Argento, or even Soavi, but he does manage to conjure an atmosphere of subdued dread and eeriness, particularly in the scenes within the wax museum, with the creepy dummies and moody lighting.

Working with Argento, Lamberto Bava and Michele Soavi had obviously taught Stivaletti how to move his camera around effectively and there are a couple of striking shots in the film, particularly the opening one when the camera pulls back from a view over firework-illuminated Paris, through a window and across a room to reveal the aftermath of a bloody murder.

The combination of alchemy with Victorian technology provides a neat twist in the tale, with the bodies of the victims, unable to move in their wax encasements due to a drug administered by the crazed Volkoff, kept alive by a communal heart. His subterranean laboratory looks like a grotesque hybrid of Frankenstein's lab and a rock video, pre-empting the look of Argento's *Phantom of the Opera*.

Stivaletti gets a little self-reflexive in some scenes, where he unveils gruesome murders only to pull the camera back to reveal the scenarios as exhibits in the museum – momentarily lifting us out of the story to consider the power of special effects.

A number of chilling moments involving children are also executed to shocking effect: a mysterious cloaked figure lures a young boy away from some other children with the promise of cotton candy, only to take him to a secluded spot in the park where Stivaletti's camera doesn't follow; implying the violence to come. After the attempted abduction of a little girl thought to be dead, the physician about to perform the autopsy realises that she is actually very much alive, her heart slowed down by a mysterious drug rendering her incapable of moving.

The climax of the film features the bewildering sight of Volkoff's true form – a cross between the Terminator and the Crypt Keeper – as he perishes in the flames of the museum in a surprise ending that doesn't make any sense.

Stivaletti was so dedicated to the project that, when he went over budget and over time, he funded the completion of the film himself and shot the remaining scenes in his own home, his special-effects studio standing in for the underground lab. He and Argento also thought it fitting to dedicate the project to Lucio Fulci.

Trivia

Apparently, a head created by Tom Savini for *Trauma* was used as a prop in the French Revolution exhibit in the wax museum.

Scarlet Diva (2000)

Directed/Written by: Asia Argento
Produced by: Dario Argento & Claudio Argento

Music by: John Hughes
Cinematographer: Frederic Fasano
Edited by: Anna Rosa Napoli AMC
Production Designer: Alessandro Rosa
Special Effects: Sergio Stivaletti
Cast: Asia Argento (Anna Battista), Jean Shepard (Kirk Vaines), Herbert Fritsch (Aaron Ulrich), Vera Gemma (Veronica), Daria Nicolodi (Anna's mother), Gianluca Arcopinto (Dr Pascuccia)

Synopsis

Actress Anna Battista appears to have it all: youth, beauty, wealth and success. However, she feels deeply lonely and frustrated and wants something more than her superficial career as an actress; she wants to become a true artist, expressing herself through writing and directing. She sets off on a self-destructive and drug-fuelled odyssey of self-discovery that leads her across Europe and on to America, meeting an assortment of eccentric and scarred individuals along the way.

Comments

Prior to *Scarlet Diva*, Asia Argento directed a number of short films and a couple of documentaries about her father and Abel Ferrara that were acclaimed enough to earn her several awards. A prolific writer too, she has penned a number of short stories and a novel, which became the cornerstone of this film, detailing her doomed relationship with a rock musician. Fiercely independent and headstrong, Asia has fought off accusations of nepotism and gone on to carve a successful and credible career away from the shadow of her father. Kitsch, subversive, trashy and irreverent, *Scarlet Diva* is her semi-autobiographical feature debut. Boasting an exceptionally brave performance from Asia herself, the film is nowhere near as self-indulgent as it could have been. Shot in an intimate, video-diary style, we witness the unfolding dramas of her life firsthand and in gory detail. Like her father, Asia bombards the audience with visually striking imagery and set pieces, held together by a vague and wandering narrative that frequently plunges into nightmarish territory. Darkly humorous and at times so surreal it's quite Lynchian, it effectively conveys Asia's ability to create a compelling story that unfurls like a sinister visual poem.

Anna's disjointed journey proves as disorientating for her as it does the viewer, sometimes rendering both parties unable to identify exactly where they are. Drug-fuelled fever-dreams and hallucinations often bleed out into Anna's reality, and at times events become so nightmarish that it's overwhelming. A number of startling set pieces really stand out, such as the languid scene where Anna is putting on make-up while gazing into her mirror, only to indignantly smear it across her face, and the scene during a photo shoot when her drugs are spiked and she nearly drowns, only to vaguely realise, half-stoned, half-conscious, that the photographers are exploiting and abusing her, photographing her in her vulnerable state. The scene in which she finds out she is pregnant is also effective as it cuts to a shot of her as a little girl, conveying her immaturity and inability to deal with her present situation.

The handheld approach was considered by Asia's father when he was shooting *Trauma*, but, as the technology was still in its infancy, he abandoned the notion. Extremely supportive of his daughter, Dario only visited the set a couple of times, preferring to give his daughter space to explore her own creativity. She claims that if she hadn't made *Scarlet Diva* she would have died creatively. Having worked with Abel Ferrara on *New Rose Hotel* (1998), Asia felt drained and was verging on agoraphobia. Writing and filming *Scarlet Diva* helped her regain control. She ditched plans to write and direct a war film, as she felt it would have required more directorial experience than she had, and concentrated instead on fashioning the *Valley of the Dolls* (1967)-themed story that became *Scarlet Diva*. She became deeply involved in the telling of her story about the trappings of fame and fortune, twisting them into an overtly grotesque mirror of her own life, portraying many people involved in the film industry as hedonistic wrecks, happily ruining their own lives and those of others.

Another trait she seems to have inherited from her father is the desire to harm her mother (Daria Nicolodi) on screen, perhaps shedding some light on the way her father was constantly doing the same by stating that she needed to 'exorcise' their relationship.

Having learned from her father about the importance of preparation while still allowing room for spontaneity, Asia takes a very experimental approach to filmmaking. From Ferrara she had learned to give actors their space and create an intimate environment with a small crew in which they could thrive; she even shot some scenes on her own to allow herself to be completely uninhibited. Asia dedicated the film to her half-sister Anna who died in a road accident prior to the making of the film.

Trivia

One of Asia's paintings, used in *The Stendhal Syndrome*, hangs on the wall in Anna's apartment. Snippets from Argento's *Phantom of the Opera* can be glimpsed on a screen in a bizarre and disturbing dream sequence.

SADISTIC SCRIPTS: ARGENTO'S WORK AS WRITER

Before directing, Argento made a name for himself writing films for others, and he frequently dabbled in genres outside of the *giallo* and horror such as Westerns, war films and psycho-sexual dramas. He soon realised, however, that his own particular speciality lay in the horror/thriller genre.

Scusi, lei e favorevole o contrario?/ Excuse me, are you For or Against? (1967)

Bizarre comedy following the exploits of a man claiming to oppose divorce because of religious reasons, all the while cheating on his wife with a variety of women and struggling to keep his increasingly hectic affairs a secret.

Directed by: Alberto Sordi
Written by: Dario Argento & Sergio Amidei

Qualcuno ha tradito/Every man is my Enemy (1967)

Existential thriller detailing a botched jewellery heist. Solidarity within the group begins to fray as each member suspects the others of betrayal. Copious bloodshed ensues.

Directed by: Franco Prosperi
Written by: Dario Argento & Raimondo Del Balzo

Les héros ne meurent jamais/Heroes Never Die (1968)

World War II drama following a crack commando team attempting to infiltrate and destroy a Nazi chemical-weapons factory in Norway.

Directed by: Maurizio Lucidi
Written by: Dario Argento

Oggi a me... domani a te!/Today it's me... Tomorrow it's you! aka Today we kill, Tomorrow we die! (1968)

Violent Spaghetti Western. After being released from jail for serving time for a crime of which he was innocent, a man forms a gang to help him seek revenge on those who committed the crime he was accused of.

Directed by: Tonino Cervi
Written by: Tonino Cervi & Dario Argento

Comandamenti per un gangster/ Commandments for a Gangster (1968)

Crime thriller following a gangster who sets out to avenge the death of his sister, who was married to a powerful rival.

Directed by: Alfio Caltabiano
Written by: Alfio Caltabiano & Dario Argento

Commandos (1968)

War drama about a group of Italian-American soldiers who infiltrate and eventually occupy a North African camp and await the arrival of their battalion. However, after an entomologist is murdered in the camp, all hell breaks loose.

Directed by: Armando Crispino
Written by: Armando Crispino, Dario Argento, Lucio Battistrada & Stefano Strucchi

La Rivoluzione sessuale/The Sexual Revolution (1968)

An Austrian psychoanalyst gathers together seven couples from different backgrounds and invites them to partake in a series of sexual orgies supposedly free from taboo and consequence.

Directed by: Riccardo Ghione
Written by: Riccardo Ghione & Dario Argento

C'era una volta il West/Once upon a Time in the West (1968)

When a woman's husband and family are murdered at the behest of railroad tycoon Mortan, she is aided by two mysterious strangers: Cheyenne and Harmonica. It soon becomes clear they both have very different motives for helping her exact revenge on her husband's killers.

Directed by: Sergio Leone
Story by: Sergio Leone, Dario Argento & Bernardo Bertolucci

Une corde, un colt/Cemetery Without Crosses (1969)

A man swears to avenge the death of his friend at the hands of a rival family in this Spaghetti Western. When he kidnaps the daughter of the said family, his friend's widow has her raped and beaten and offers her back to the family in exchange for the burial of her dead husband. The family decide to avenge the molestation of their daughter.

Directed by: Robert Hossein
Written by: Robert Hossein, Dario Argento & Claude Desailly

Metti una sera a cena/The Love Circle (1969)

The morals of three men and two women are put to the test when they engage in a series of partner-swapping sexual liaisons in this comedy-morality play.

Directed by: Giuseppe Patroni Griffi
Written by: Giuseppe Patroni Griffi, Dario Argento & Carlo Carunchio

Probabilita zero/Possibility Zero (1969)

War-time thriller following the exploits of a misfit commando squad attempting to infiltrate and occupy a Nazi fortress with the aid of a recycled torpedo.

Directed by: Maurizio Lucidi
Written by: Dario Argento, Giuseppe Mangione & Vittoriano Vighi

La Legione dei dannati/Legion of the Damned aka Battle of the Commandos (1969)

An army colonel, bitter because of his previous troop's forced suicide mission, helps prepare a group of convicted criminals for D-Day in this war drama.

Directed by: Umberto Lenzi
Written by: Dario Argento, Rolf Grieminger & Eduardo Manzanos Brochero

Un Esercito di cinque uomini/The Five Man Army (1969)

Spaghetti Western. During the Mexican Revolution, a group of old acquaintances hatch a plan to rob vast amounts of gold from a train that is heavily guarded by armed forces and passes through several military checkpoints.

Directed by: Don Taylor & Italo Zingarelli
Written by: Dario Argento & Marc Richards

La Stagione dei sensi/Season of the Senses (1969)

After murdering his overbearing mistress, a wealthy recluse engages in a series of humiliating, psychologically charged and sexually explicit games with several young women in his secluded island home.

Directed by: Massimo Franciosa
Written by: Barbara Alberti, Dario Argento, Franco Ferrari & Peter Kintzel

Così sia/Man Called Amen (1972)

Comedy-Western following the misadventures of two simple-minded bandits as they team up with a philosopher to rob a bank.

Directed by: Alfio Caltabiano
Written by: Alfio Caltabiano, Dario Argento & Adriano Bolzoni

BIBLIOGRAPHY

Fuchs, Christian, *Bad Blood: An Illustrated Guide to Psycho Cinema*, England: Creation Books, 2002

Gallant, Chris (ed), *Art of Darkness: The Cinema of Dario Argento*, Surrey: FAB Press, 2001 (First published 2000)

Hardy, Phil (ed), *The Aurum Encyclopaedia: Horror*, London: Aurum Press Ltd, 1996 (First published 1985)

Jones, Alan, *Profondo Argento: The Man, the Myths & the Magic*, Surrey: FAB Press, 2004

Koven, Mikel J, *La Dolce Morte: Vernacular Cinema and the Italian Giallo Film*, Lanham: Scarecrow Press, 2006

McDonagh, Maitland, *Broken Mirrors/Broken Minds: The Dark Dreams of Dario Argento*, New York: Citadel Press, 1994

Mendik, Xavier, *Tenebrae*, Wiltshire: Flicks Books, 2000

Odell, Colin & Michelle Le Blanc, *Horror Films*, Herts: Kamera Books, 2007

Palmerini, Luca, *Spaghetti Nightmares: Italian Fantasy-Horrors as Seen Through the Eyes of their Protagonists*, US: Fantasma Books, 1996

REFERENCES

1 Review of *Tenebrae* from *Films & Filming* (Sept 1983)
2 Clover, Carol J, 'Her Body, Himself: Gender in the Slasher Film' in Barry Keith Grant (ed), *The Dread of Difference: Gender and the Horror Film* (University of Texas Press, 1996), p 77
3 Ibid, p 77
4 Jones, Alan, *Profondo Argento: The Man, the Myths & the Magic* (FAB Press, 2004), p 195
5 Fuchs, Christian, *Bad Blood: An Illustrated Guide to Psycho Cinema* (Creation Books, 2002), p 295
6 Knapp, Laurence F (ed), *Brian De Palma: Interviews – Conversations with Film-makers Series* (University Press of Mississippi, 2003), p 143
7 Quotation from *Dario Argento: An Eye for Horror* (2000) (TV), dir Leon Ferguson
8 Fuchs, op cit, p 292
9 Ibid, p 293
10 Gallant, Chris (ed), *Art of Darkness: The Cinema of Dario Argento* (FAB Press, 2001), p 111
11 Grainger, Julian, 'Deep Red' in Gallant, Chris (ed), *Art of Darkness: The Cinema of Dario Argento* (FAB Press, 2001) p 117
12 Interview with Sean Keller, *Cinefantastique*, http://cinefantastiqueonline.com/2009/05/26/yellow-fever-sean-keller-on-writing-giallo-for-dario-argento/
13 Ibid
14 Ibid
15 Interview with Marco Werba, www.littlewhitelies.co.uk/interviews/marco-werba

You have been reading a book about Dario Argento.

INDEX

kamera BOOKS

ESSENTIAL READING FOR ANYONE INTERESTED IN FILM AND POPULAR CULTURE

Tackling a wide range of subjects from prominent directors, popular genres and current trends through to cult films, national cinemas and film concepts and theories. Kamera Books come complete with complementary DVDs packed with additional material, including feature films, shorts, documentaries and interviews.

Silent Cinema
Brian J. Robb

A handy guide to the art of cinema's silent years in Hollywood and across the globe.

978-1-904048-63-3 **£9.99**

Dalí, Surrealism and Cinema
Elliott H. King

This book surveys the full range of Dalí's eccentric activities with(in) the cinema.

978-1-904048-90-9 **£9.99**

East Asian Cinema
David Carter

An ideal reference work on all the major directors, with details of their films.

978-1-904048-68-8 **£9.99**

David Lynch
Colin Odell & Michelle Le Blanc

Examines Lynch's entire works, considering the themes, motifs and stories behind his incredible films.

978-1-84243-225-9 **£9.99**